IN SEARCH OF ANGES DEACH

OUR FAMILY SEARCH FOR ANCESTORS

PATRICIA ANN DEACH

authorHOUSE®

AuthorHouse™
1663 Liberty Drive
Bloomington, IN 47403
www.authorhouse.com
Phone: 1-800-839-8640

Published by AuthorHouse   11/21/2014

ISBN: 978-1-4969-5492-3 (sc)
ISBN: 978-1-4969-5491-6 (e)

Library of Congress Control Number: 2014920877

This book is printed on acid-free paper.

DEDICATION

I dedicate this book to my husband and sons, and to those that I have not met, but are likewise looking for where they fit into this family. It is always nice to know whom we came from and where we may get our personality and perhaps our looks. I give many thanks to the family members that had led me along the way with information to help me in writing this book. I have always tried to verify the information I have, to make sure that it is correct. I am sure some mistakes are sure to happen on the way to writing this down, please forgive me. Family stories I have gathered from Ancestry and family members gives a great picture of the Deach immigrants, and the footprint they left behind.

DNA RESULTS

Merle Deach
Great Grandson of Anges Deach

This test given through Ancestry DNA Genetic Ethnicity.

Central European----61%
Southern European--13%
British Isles-------------12%
These results figure out to be as follows:
Europe West ----------39%
Ireland-----------------30%
Italy/Greece-----------12%
Finland/N.W. Russia—8%
Trace results:
Africa<1%
Asia<1%
Uncertain just under 14%

WELCOME TO YOU

Written by John and Louise Deach

So glad you could be with us today. Our apologies for any errors in names and dates. We did the best we could. John and Louise.

Date of December 2, 1984 family reunion at Uncle John's home in Centralia Washington.

Not everyone came, but it was nice meeting Merle's family. The boys still remember Uncle John's old car and the one arm bandit slot machine he had downstairs. Aunt Maxine age 69 yrs- Aunt Ruth age 55 yrs- Uncle John of course and wife Louise- Darlene M. Deach Bower- Tom Bower- Terri Bianchi- Kimberly Baird, 23 yrs- Joey 6 yrs- jarred 3 yrs- Jolie 1 yr. and of course Merle Robin Doug Carl and Jeremy Deach.

Everyone was given a book on the history of family members, as they knew it. At the very back of the book was a place for autographs, and the list of family names above are the ones who signed our book. This was long before personal computers were common in every ones homes. I remember Aunt Ruth telling me that this book would be something we would want to keep, and it may not be important at the time but it may be in the future. How right she was. Having joined Ancestry in 2008 the information I am about to put down came from the book we received at the Deach Family Reunion. It does contain errors that will be corrected when we get the updated information from my research. I am putting the Welcome to You chapter at the beginning of this book because of all the work that had been done by a family member, but more importantly, it was great as a reference to turn to.

I will start this out with Anges Deach and his wife Doris Kelly. Their children's names are:

(1.) THOMAS DEACH
(2.) BESS
(3.) WILLIAM DEACH was born April 17, 1875. Died from, Myocarditis, Uremia and Diabetes. No date was given, was buried at Mt. View Cemetery Centralia Washington April 5, 1947.
(4.) THERESA DEACH CARTER, her children:

a.   Pearl Carter Livernash, born November 29, 19? Park Rapid Minnesota. Died May 13, 1977. Her children are:

1.   Edna Carter Gunderson
2.   Earl Carter
3.   Lyle Livernash
4.   Glen Livernash

(5.) LINDA DEACH WINTERS, she had the following children:

a.   Velda Winters Laudry (Earnest)

(6.) JAMES A. DEACH married Ethel (Adams) second wife Peg. James had the following children:

a.   Freda Maude Deach Peterson, husband's name Ira Oscar. They had the following children:

1.   Florence Peterson Lowland. Born February 23, 1923.
2.   Vivian L. Peterson Nessel
3.   Donald Peterson born April 2 1924. Wife Anna May.
4.   Robert I Peterson born April 2, 1924.

(7.) FINLEY MALCOM DEACH born April 10, 1884, and died October 4, 1945 from cardiac, asthma, Whidbey Island Washington. Married to Mabel Mae Monte. She passed away October 8, 1943 (57) from Diabetes, Whidbey Island Washington. They had the following children:

a.   Walter Bersch died from Kidney stones September 1935 Spokane Washington.
b.   Ardella (Dot) Willmina Bersch, Landrum, Hardenbrook. Born in Minneapolis Minnesota January 16, 1908. She had the following children:

1.   Vivian Deloris Hardenbrook born June 18, 1925 Bellingham Washington.
2.   Jack Smith Hardenbrook born December 12, 1928 Dietrick Idaho, died September 22, 1963.

c.   Hazel Mae Deach Land Hawkins born March 6, 1915 Graylin Minnesota. Hazel married to Thomas John Hawkins June 25, 1949 Grandview Washington. They had the following children:

1.   Beverly Mae Land died February 1933 Grandview Washington.
2.   Eugene Arthur Land born, August 28, 1935 Prosser Washington.

4

3. Glen Walter Land born March 7, 1938 Grandview Washington.
4. Warren Thomas Hawkins Land- Stepson born July 1, 1941 Yakima Washington.
5. Sandra Ellen Hawkins Anderson stepdaughter born June 21, 1943 Tacoma Washington.

d. Thomas R. Deach born April 27, 1917 married to Betty. They had the following children:

1. Joann
2. John
3. Thomas R. Deach Jr.

e. Alfred Monte Deach born February 24, 1919 and died January 20, 1973 (53 yrs). Buried Greenwood cemetery Renton Washington. Married to Dorothy Dahm and they had the following children:

1. Billie Dee Deach (by first wife)
2. Merle Thomas
3. Allen
4. Gary
5. Marshall
6. Wilbur
7. Carl Malcom Deach deceased born June 19, 1954.
8. Sherman Royal Deach born May 30, 1961.
9. Sharon Deach Segebartt

f. Maxine Marcella Deach Baird, born October 30, 1921 Bellingham Washington. Married to Allan Baird November 18, 1937 Prosser Washington. They had the following children:

1. Larry Baird born May 31, 1938 Grandview Washington.

2. Marlene Baird Bianchi born July 6, 1941 Oak Harbor Washington.

3. Kimberly Baird born March 6, 1961 Seattle Washington.

g. John Angus Deach born September 14, 1925 Bellingham Washington. Married Louise Doris Patenaude October 3, 1948, First Christian Church, Centralia Washington, they had the following children:

1. John A Deach Jr. born January 10, 1952 Chehalis Washington.

2. James Finley Deach born April 17, 1954 Chehalis Washington.

3. Larry Lee Deach born September 24, 1956 Chehalis Washington.

h. Ruth Marion Deach Dismukes Treser, born August 12, 1929 Milwaukee Wisconsin. Married George Dismukes April 12, 1950. Married Calvin C. Treser divorced. Ruth had the following children:

1. Lonnett Dyann Deach born August 25, 1946 Spokane Washington.

October 11, 2014

I am sure there are mistakes that have been made in their researching the family. I hope that I will have all names and dates corrected through using Ancestry. Aunt Ruth had told me (Robin) that the information they had collected may not be important at the time, (Family Reunion) but may be important in the future. How right she was. The foundation of this book was based on their work.

ANGES DEACH

Nov 6, 1842 - Sept 21, 1914
Son of AUGUST DEACH and MARTHA SCHULTZ

I am starting this out with the research I have found and believe it to be true. There has been some question on the spelling of Anges's name. I have found it spelled as Anges as well as Angus. I sent for Anges's death certificate hoping to clear up many questions that I had regarding his name and who his parents were. The death certificate shows his name spelled Anges, it also showed his parents names as August Deach and Martha Schultz. Thomas, his son was the one that had given the information and sign the death certificate.

Anges Deach was born in Prussia now Deutschland, Germany, date 06 Nov 1842. His death was 19 Sept 1914 in St Paul, Ramsey, Minnesota, USA. He is intern in Roselawn Cemetery, Roseville, St Paul, Ramsey, Minnesota, section A block D lot 106 space 1.

The following information was sent to me from Kathe Deach; Thomas Deach was an ancestor of her husband's.

Death Announcement

Anges, a former resident of this vicinity, died Saturday Morning at the home of his son in St Paul, where he had made his home for the past two to three years. The Funeral was held there Monday, State of Minnesota, County of Ramset. Ss.

In Probate Court

In the matter of providing the Alleged Last Will and Testament of Anges Deach. Decedent. The State of Minnesota to all whom it may concern:

Whereas, Thomas Angus Deach, of the City of St Paul, and State of Minnesota, has delivered to the Probate Court, of the County of Ramsey, an instrument in writing purporting to be the last will and testament of Anges Deach, late of Ramsey County, Minnesota, decedent, and filed therewith his petition to said Probate Court, praying that the said instrument may prove and admitted to probate and that letters testamentary be granted thereon to George C. Sudheimer.

It is ordered, that said petition be heard and that all persons interested in said matter be cited and required to appear before this Court on Monday, the 19th day of October, 1914 at 10 o'clock A.M. or as soon thereafter as said matter can be heard, at the Probate Court Rooms in the Court House, in the City of St Paul in said County, and show cause if any they have, why said petition should not be granted and said will admitted to probate and that this citation be served by the publication thereof in The West Saint Paul Times according to law, and by mailing a copy of this citation at least 11 days before said day of hearing, to each of the heirs, devisees, legatees of said decedent whose name and addresses are known and appear from the files of this court. Witness the Judge of said Court, this 24h day of September A.D. 1914.

E.W. RAZILL'E Judge of Probate. (Seal of Probate Court.) Attest: F.W. Gosewisch, Clerk of Probate. Geo. Sudheimer, Attorney.

The 1861 Census of Canada shows his birth as being born in Germany 1842, and that he lived in Townsend, Norfolk, Canada West, Canada.

1868 age 26, he arrived into the United States.

Federal Census 1870 Age 28 resided in Portland, Cerro Gordo, Iowa, USA.

February 22, 1874 Marriage to Malinda E. Kelley Mason City.

Federal Census 1880 age 38, he resided in Portland, Cerro Gordo, Iowa, USA.

Federal Census 1900 Census shows Anges divorced and residing in Benton & Summer Townships, Spink, South Dakota.

1905 Age 63 Residence South Dakota, USA. Marital Status: Divorced

1914 Sept 19, Age 71 Death. Roseville, St Paul, Ramsey Minnesota.

Minnesota, Death Index, 1908-2002 gives one citation that provides evidence for name and death.

Malinda E. Kelley born 1854 in Ucon Ontario Canada.

Parents James R. Kelley 1825 – 1893 Elizabeth Curtis born 1830. Parents are questionable. Needs more research.

1866 Age 12 Arrived into the United States.

1874 Age 20 married Anges Deach Mason City Iowa.

Federal Census 1900 Age 46 Residence Detroit Village, Becker, Minnesota Shows Malinda married, but above in census on Anges shows he's divorced. This must be the year they divorced.

Federal Census 1910 Age 56 Residence Licking, Whatcom, Washington, USA. Shows Malinda married wife to head of house. (Second) husband Allen W. McGavin.

1913 Age 59 Malinda resided in Bellingham Washington, USA.

April 2, 1918 Malinda Age 64, Death Yelm Washington, USA.

Burial Pioneer Cemetery Yelm Washington. There is no longer a marker on her grave; they had a prairie fire, which destroyed many markers as well as the papers of the intern.

Malinda's second husband Allen McGavin was born in Canada and this was his second marriage.

Allen McGavin died November 22, 1915, Sedro Woolley Washington, USA. Age 67.

Children of Anges and Malinda Deach as follows:

WILLIAM ANDREW DEACH Born April 1875 in Iowa, USA. Death 05 Apr 1947 Centralia, Lewis County, Washington. Burial Pioneer Cemetery Centralia, Lewis County Washington, USA. Section 18 plot 49.

THERESA M DEACH Born 9 Oct 1876 Iowa, USA. Death Age 45 Yelm, Thurston, Washington, USA.

THOMAS EDWARD DEACH Born 17 Mar 1878 Nora Springs, Floyd, Iowa, USA. Death 11 Apr 1950 St Paul, Ramsey,

Minnesota section 8 lot 406 Roselawn Cemetery St. Paul, Ramsey Minnesota, USA.

JAMES R DEACH Born 29 May 1880 Nora Springs, Floyd, Iowa, USA. Death 06 Oct 1947 Bellingham, Whatcom County, Washington, USA.

FINLEY MALCOM DEACH Born 10 Apr 1884 Spink, South Dakota, USA. Death 04 Oct 1945 Langley, Island County, Washington, USA.

MELINDA E DEACH Born 08 Oct 1886 South Dakota, USA. Death 16 Mar 1937 Laurel Heights, Snohomish, Washington, USA. Burial Marysville, Snohomish County, Washington, USA.

HELEN R DEACH Born 08 Apr 1888

BETSEY MAE DEACH Born 05 Mar 1890, Becker Minnesota, USA.

WILLIAM ANDREW DEACH

SON of ANGES

Born April 17 1875 Iowa, USA.

Death April 5 1947 Centralia, Lewis County, Washington, USA.

Burial Pioneer Cemetery Centralia, Lewis, Washington, USA. Plot: Section 18, Plot 49. Pioneer Cemetery is directly behind Mountain View Cemetery.

1900 Federal Census-William living in Detroit, Becker, Minnesota, USA. Age 25 single. Relation to head of house stepson.

Federal Census 1910- Residence Bellingham Ward 3, Whatcom, Washington, USA. Age 38 Single, stepson to head of house.

Federal Census 1930- Residence West Prosser, Benton, Washington, USA. Lodger age 54.

1935 Age 60 residence West Prosser, Benton, Washington, USA.

Federal Census 1940- Age 64 single relationship to head of house lodger. West Prosser, Benton, Washington, USA.

1947 Death Centralia, Washington, USA.

U.S. World War 1 Draft Registration Cards, 1917-1918 one citation provides evidence for name, birth, and residence.

William remained single.

THERESA M DEACH

Daughter of Anges Deach

Born 9 OCT 1896 Iowa, USA.

Death 1941 Yelm, Thurston, Washington, USA.

Burial Yelm Public Cemetery, Thurston County, Washington, USA.

Theresa was married to Walter B Carter, born in England about 1865. He arrived in the USA in 1874 age 9. He died July 20, 1934 in Thurston, Washington, USA. Buried next to Theresa.

1910 Census shows him married and living in Goshen, Whatcom, Washington, USA. He was born in 1862, so Theresa married a much older man. His parents were William Carter and unknown Seymour.

1920 Federal Census shows Theresa living in Yelm, Thurston, Washington, USA.

Theresa and Walter had the following children:

(A.) Pearl M Carter born 29 Nov 1900 Minnesota, USA

Death 13 May 1977 Olympia, Washington, USA.

1910 Federal Census Age 9 living in Licking, Whatcom, Washington, USA.

1920 Federal Census Age 19 living in Yelm, Thurston, Washington, USA.

Pearl married Elmer Francis Livernash, Elmer was born about 1897 Wisconsin, USA.

1935 Pearl and Elmer were living in Yelm, Washington, USA.

1940 Federal Census Shows Pearl age 39 and Elmer age 43 living in Yelm, Washington, USA.

1942 Residing in Yelm, Washington, USA.

14 Dec 1959 Elmer died at the age of 62 Yelm, Washington, USA.

Burial Tumwater, Washington, USA. I believe most likely buried next to Pearl.

Pearl and Elmer had the following children:

1.   Lyle Livernash born about 1932 Washington, USA.

1935 resided in Yelm, Washington, USA. Age 3

1940 Federal Census age 8 residence Yelm, Washington, USA.

2.   Glen Livernash born about 1934 Washington, USA.

1935 age one resided in Yelm, Washington, USA.

1940 Federal Census Age 6 resides in Yelm, Washington, USA.

(B.)   Earl E Carter born about 1904 Minnesota, USA.

June 1925 age one residence Woodside.

1910 Federal Census living in Licking, Whatcom, Washington, USA.

1920 Federal Census Residence Yelm, Washington, USA.

1930 Federal Census Residence Anacortes, Skagit, Washington, USA.

1940 Federal Census Residence Bad Hills, Thurston, Washington, USA. Age 36 marital status divorced. Wife unknown.

(C.)   Esther E Carter born about 1906 North Dakota.

1910 Federal Census age 4 residence Licking, Whatcom, Washington, USA.

1920 Federal Census age 14 resides in Yelm, Washington, USA.

September 26, 1928 Ester marries James O Wright in Whatcom, Washington, USA.

1930 Federal Census age 24 living with husband in Anacortes, Skagit, Washington, USA.

1940 Federal Census age 34 living in Anacortes, Skagit, Washington, USA.

Esther and James had the following children:

1.   David L Wright born about 1921, USA.

1930 Federal Census age 9 residing in Anacortes, Washington, USA.

2.   Ralph E Wright born about 1922 USA.

1930 Federal Census age 8 residing in Anacortes, Washington, USA.

3.   Jeane M Wright born about 1928 USA.

1930 Federal Census age 2 residing in Anacortes, Washington, USA.

(D.) Edna M Carter born 22 Feb 1909 Bellingham, Washington, USA.

1910 Federal Census age 1 residing in Licking, Washington, USA.

1920 Federal Census age 11 residence Yelm, Washington, USA.

December 19, 1929 married Carl A Gunderson. Thurston County, Washington, USA.

1929 resided in Tacoma, Washington, USA.

1930 Federal Census age 21 resided in Tacoma, Washington, USA.

1934 age 25 resided in Tacoma, Washington, USA.

1935 Federal Census age 26 resided in Tacoma, Washington, USA.

1951 Age 42 residing in Tacoma, Washington, USA.

1955 age 46 residing in Tacoma, Washington, USA.

1958 age 49 residing in Tacoma Washington, USA.

October 22, 1981 Death, age 72 Tacoma, Washington, USA.

Washington Death Index, 1940-1996 one citation provides evidence for name, birth and death.

Washington, Birth 1883-1935, one citation provides evidence for name and birth.

Edna and Carl had the following children:

1. Robert L Gunderson born About 1932 Washington, USA.

1935 age 3 resided in Tacoma, Washington, USA.

1940 Federal Census age 8 resides in Tacoma, Washington, USA.

THOMAS EDWARD DEACH

Son of Anges Deach

Born March 17, 1878, Nora Springs, Floyd, Iowa, USA.

Death April 11, 1950, St Paul, Ramsey, Minnesota, USA.

Burial- Roseville, Ramsey County, Minnesota, USA. Roselawn Cemetery St Paul, Ramsey, Minnesota section 8 lot 406 sp 1.

1900 Federal census shows Thomas living in River Falls, Red Lake, Minnesota. Age 22 and single.

1905 June 8 age 27 still living in River Falls, Red Lake, Minnesota, USA.

1910 Federal Census Thomas is age 32, married living in Minneapolis Ward 2, Hennepin, Minnesota.

1920 Federal Census age 42; married St Paul ward 10, Ramsey, Minnesota, USA.

1930 Federal Census age 52 widowed. St Paul, Ramsey, Minnesota, USA.

1940 April 1 age 62 windowed relation to head of house Father-In-Law.

1950 Federal Census April 11, Death age 72.

Thomas married to Minnie Kopperud. She was born 1880 in Polk County, Minnesota, USA. She died December 17, 1927 in St Paul, Ramsey Minnesota. Her parents were Peter J Jonsavin Kopperud, and Karen Jorgensdatter 1847-1885.

At the age of 15, she lived in Hubbard, Polk, Minnesota, USA. She was single and living as a boarder.

1905 June 8 age 25 she lived in River Falls, Red Lake, Minnesota, USA.

1910 Federal Census age 30 married to head of house, living in Minneapolis Ward 2, Hennepin Minnesota, USA.

1920 Federal Census age 40 married to head of house. Living in St Paul, Ward 10, Ramsey, Minnesota, USA.

December 17, 1927 she passed away and was buried next to her husband Thomas in Roselawn Cemetery. Roseville, Ramsey, Minnesota. Sp 2 lot 406.

Thomas and Minnie had the following children:

(A.) Myrtle Deach born about 1906 in Minnesota, USA.

1910 Federal Census shows Myrtle age 4 daughter to head of house. Living in Minneapolis Ward 2, Hennepin, Minnesota, USA.

1920 Federal Census age 14, daughter to head of house, living in St Paul, Ramsey, Minnesota, USA.

(B.)   Russell Palmer Deach born December 7, 1910, St Paul, Ramsey, Minnesota, USA.

Death, December 26, 1966 Hennepin, Minnesota, USA. Burial Roselawn Cemetery, Roseville, Ramsey, Minnesota section 8, lot 65, sp2 age 58.

1910 Federal Census age 2, son to head of house, living in Minneapolis Ward 2, Hennepin Minnesota, USA.

1920 Federal Census age 11, son to head of house, living in St Paul Ward 10, Ramsey, Minnesota, USA

1930 Federal Census age 22 single, son to head of house.

1937 Russell age 28, living in St Paul, Minnesota.

December 26, 1966 Hennepin, Minnesota, USA. Russell passed away age 57.

Russell was married to Dorothy M Winship, she was born December 7, 1910 St Paul, Ramsey, Minnesota, USA. Daughter of Alfred Franklin Winship 1879-1947 and Rosalie Anna Schiffmann 1877-1970.

May 15, 2005 Dorothy passed away in Jasper Pickens Georgia. Burial Roselawn Cemetery, Roseville, Ramsey, Minnesota, section 8 lot 65 age 94.

1920 Federal Census age 10 daughter to head of house, St Paul Ward 10, Ramsey, Minnesota, USA.

1930 Federal Census age 20 St Paul, Ramsey, Minnesota, USA. Daughter to head of house.

1935 age 25, she resided in El Monte, Ca.

1937 age 27 Residence St Paul, Minnesota, USA.

U.S. Social Security Death Index 1935-2014 one citation gives evidence for name, death and birth.

Russell and Dorothy had the following children:

1.   Eugene Stanley Deach. Born February 7, 1935 St Paul, Ramsey, Minnesota, USA.

May 9, 1941 he passed away in Ramsey, Minnesota, USA.

Minnesota Birth Index, 1935-2002 one citation provides evidence for name and birth.

Eugene is buried in Roselawn Cemetery, Roseville, Ramsey, Minnesota, USA. Section 8 lot 65 sp 1 age 6.

2.   James R Deach, born March 4, 1939 St Paul, Ramsey, Minnesota.

Death August 21, 2009 age 70, in Brainerd, Crow Wing, Minnesota, USA.

Last known address of James was 30009 Alpharetta Fulton Georgia.

U.S. Public Records Index, Volume 1 about James R Deach gives date of birth, phone number and last four addresses. Obituary was shown in the Atlanta Journal Constitution Atlanta, Georgia, USA.

James was married to Janice N. Pamrueh in Minnesota. They had the following children Chris, Rose, Rochelle, Kevin and six grandchildren.

(C.)   Isabelle M Deach born May 10, 1917 Minnesota USA.

February 14, 2005 passed away in St Paul, Minnesota USA. Buried Roseville, Ramsey County Minnesota, USA.

1920 Federal Census age 3 lived in St Paul Ward 10, Ramsey, Minnesota, USA.

1930 Federal Census age 13 lived in St Paul, Ramsey, Minnesota, USA. Daughter to head of house.

1940 Federal Census April 1 age 23 married to head of house.

Isabelle was married to Clement E. Barnes, date of marriage unknown. His parent were Edward Barnes 1881-unknown and Violet unknown 1890-unknown.

Clement was born December 6, 1913 Minnesota, USA.

1920 Federal Census age 7 residence St Paul, Ramsey, Minnesota, son to head of house.

1930 Federal Census age 17 Residence St Paul, Ramsey, Minnesota, USA.

1935 age 22 residence St Paul, Ramsey, Minnesota, USA.

1940 Federal Census Residence St Paul, Ramsey, Minnesota, USA married and is head of house. This census shows Thomas living with them.

1941 age 28 residing in St Paul, Ramsey, Minnesota, USA.

Minnesota Death Index 1908-2002 one citation gives evidence for name, birth and death.

Isabelle and Clement had the following children:

Patricia Ann Deach

1.   Judith May Barnes born June 17, 1939 Ramsey, Minnesota, USA.

1940 Federal Census residence St Paul, Ramsey, Minnesota, USA.

1962 May 22 1925 Marriage to Peter A Brandt Ramsey Minnesota, USA.

1928 Residence Jamestown, New York, USA.

1993 age 54, Judith resided in St Paul, Minnesota, USA.

JAMES R DEACH

Son of Anges

Born May 29, 1880 Nora Springs, Iowa, USA.

Died October 6, 1947 age 67, Bellingham, Whatcom, Washington, USA.

Buried Bellingham, Whatcom County, Washington, USA.

1899 Marriage to Ethel A Adams. She was born July 1883 Minnesota, USA.

She was 16 when she married James and he was 19. Her parents were Ardillo Clancy Adams and Anna Eliza King.

1900 Federal Census Residence River Falls, Red Lake, Minnesota, USA Married

1910 Federal Census age 30 Residence Bellingham, Ward 3, Whatcom, Washington, USA. Married.

1920 Federal Census age 40 Residence Marietta, Whatcom, Washington, USA.

1930 Federal Census age 50 Residence Marietta, Whatcom, Washington, USA.

1935 age 55 residing in Marietta, Whatcom, Washington, USA.

1936 age 56 Residence Bellingham, Washington, USA.

1940 Federal Census age 59 Residence Marietta, Washington, USA.

1941 age 61 residing in Bellingham, Washington, USA.

1942 age 62 Residence Bellingham, Washington, USA.

1947 Washington Death Index, 1940-1996 one citation provides evidence for name, birth and death.

Ethel passed away in 1945 at the age of 62.

James and Ethel had the following children:

(A.) FREDA A DEACH born about 1901 Minnesota.

1910 Federal Census age 9 living in Bellingham Ward 3, Whatcom, Washington, USA.

July 4, 1919 age 18, she married Ira O Peterson in Whatcom, Washington, USA. Ira was born 1895 Minnesota, USA.

1920 Federal Census age 19 marital status married. Relation to head of house, daughter.

1930 Federal Census age 29 living in Marietta, Whatcom, Washington, USA.

1935 age 34, residing in Marietta, Whatcom, Washington, USA.

1940 Federal Census age 39 resides in Marietta, Whatcom, Washington, USA. Married to head of house.

February 17, 1945 Death, Bellingham, Whatcom, Washington, USA.

Burial Bellingham, Washington, USA.

Washington Death Index, 1883-1960 one citation provides evidence for name, birth and death.

Freda and Ira had the following children:

1.   Vivian Lillian Peterson born about 1921 Washington, USA.

1930 Federal Census age 9 residing in Marietta, Washington USA.

1935 age 14 residing in Marietta, Washington, USA,

 1940 Federal Census age 19 resides in Marietta, Washington, USA.

1954 resides in Everett, Washington, USA.

 Vivian married Clifford Nessel. He was born April 10, 1920 Bellingham, Washington, USA.

 His parents were Joseph Nessel and Minnie Nessel.

Vivian and Clifford had the following children:

a.   Sally Nessel born March 2, 1945. Sally married Jerry
       Swalling. They had one son Gary.
b.   Joe Nessel born July 11, 1945.U.S. Public Records Index,
       Volume 1 shows Joe being born August 11, 1945 residing
       in Seattle, Washington, USA.

2.   Florence R Peterson born April 1923 Washington, USA.

1930 Federal Census age 7 resides in Marietta, Washington, USA.

1935 age 12 residing in Marietta, Washington, USA.

1940 Federal Census age 16 resides in Marietta, Washington, USA.

Nevada Death Index, 1980-2012 one citation provided evidence for name, birth and death.

Washington Marriage Records, 1865-2004 one citation provides evidence for name and marriage.

September 27, 1942 age 19 Florence married John Lowland in Whatcom County, Washington, USA.

1996 age 73 residence Reno, Washoe, Nevada, USA.

October 13, 2009 death age 86. Reno, Nevada, USA.

John Lowland death December 1, 1970.

Florence and John had the following Children:

c.   Leon Lowland
d.   Steven Lowland

3.   Robert Ira Peterson born April 2, 1924 Bellingham, Washington, USA.

1930 Federal Census age 6 residing in Marietta, Washington, USA.

1935 age 11 Residing in Marietta, Washington, USA.1940 Federal Census age 15 residence Marietta, Washington, USA.

1948 age 24 resides in Bellingham, Washington, USA.

December 31, 1991 age 67 death.

Burial Ferndale, Washington, USA.

Robert married Wilma Jean Nattress. She was born about 1926, they had the following children:

a.   Brad Peterson.
b.   Larry Peterson.
c.   Richard Peterson.
d.   Brian John Peterson born November 17, 1961 Bellingham, Washington, USA.

1993 age 32 resided in Bellingham, Washington, USA.

August 4, 1997 age 35 Death, Bellingham, Washington, USA.

U.S. Social Security Death Index, 1935-2014 one citation provides evidence for name, death and birth.

4.   Donald James Peterson born January 7, 1926 Bellingham Ward 1, Washington, USA.

1930 Federal Census age 4 Residence Marietta, Washington, USA.

1935 age 9 residing in Marietta, Washington, USA.

1940 Federal Census age 14 residence Marietta, Washington, USA.

1993 age 67 resides in Seattle, Washington, USA.

November 20 2012 Death age 86.

Donald married Anna May. They had the following children:

1. Neal Alan
2. Christopher James Peterson born March 16, 1953.

U.S. Public Records Index, Volume 2 Record provides evidence for Christopher.

3. Darrell John Peterson born March 3, 1956.

(B.) DELBERT ARDILLO DEACH born July 4 1904 Bellingham, Washington, USA.

1910 Federal Census age 6 living in Bellingham Ward 3 Whatcom, Washington, USA.

1920 Federal Census age 16 shows him living in Bellingham Ward 2, Washington, USA.

1924 age 20, he was living in Bellingham, Washington.

September 5, 1925 age 21 he married Maybelle Maria Burgess, Skagit, Washington, USA.

Her parents names Fred S. Bargess born 1878 and Martha Josephine Bates, born 1883-1961.

1930 Federal Census age 26 married and is head of house, living in Marietta, Whatcom, Washington, USA.

1940 Federal Census age 38 living in Lake City, King, Washington, USA. Shows occupation Truck Driver, Mechanic. Highest grade completed, elementary school, 8th grade.

Delbert Ardillo married a second time, her name Shirley Anderson 1921-2007.

August 7, 1958 Death age 54, Everett (Rural), Snohomish, Washington, USA.

Delbert and Maria had the following children:

1.   Donald A Deach born June 17, 1926, in Washington, USA.

1930 Federal Census age 4 shows him living in Marietta, Whatcom, Washington, USA.

1935 age 9, he was living in Seattle Washington, USA.

1940 Federal Census age 13, he was living in Preshastin, Chelan, Washington, USA.

2.   Dorothy A Deach born about 1928 Washington, USA.

1930 Federal Census age 2 residence Marietta, Whatcom, Washington, USA.

1940 Federal Census age 12 resided in Pershastin, Chelan, Washington, USA.

3.   Joyce E Deach born about 1931 in Washington, USA.

1930 Federal Census residence Marietta, Washington, USA.

1940 Federal Census age 10 residence Preshastin, Chelan, Washington, USA.

Joyce married Donald Tisdale.

November 18, 1969 age 43, he married Maria Isabelle Lewis, in Whatcom County, Washington, USA.

1991 age 65, he resided in Everett, Washington, USA.

April 23/ 1992 age 65 Death, Auburn Washington, USA.

Washington Death Index, 1935-1996, one citation provides evidence for name, birth and death.

Washington Marriage records 1865-2004 one citation provides evidence for name and marriage.

(C.) JAMES B DEACH born May 25, 1905 Bellingham, Washington, USA.

1910 Federal Census age 5 Residence Bellingham ward 3, Whatcom, Washington, USA.

1920 Federal Census age 15 Residence Bellingham ward 2, Whatcom, Washington, USA.

1930 Federal Census age 25 Residence Seattle, Washington, USA. This census shows James worked with drywall. This census also shows James was a tanner of Fox hides.

James was married twice. First wife Nellie La Rocque, marriage date October 7, 1930 Clark Washington. Found no children from this marriage.

Second wife Helen l Hedlund. Date for this marriage August 16, 1941 city of Bellingham, Washington, USA.

1940 Federal Census age 35 residence Blue, Jackson, Missouri, USA.

January 2 1954 age 49 death. Seattle Washington, USA.

Could not find any descendants.

James occupation Beer Parlor and Restaurant

(D.)   Margaret E Deach born about 1916 Washington, USA.

1920 Federal Census age 4 Residence Bellingham ward 2, Whatcom, Washington, USA.

1930 Federal Census age 14 residence Marietta, Whatcom, Washington, USA.

1935 age 19 lived in Seattle, King, Washington, USA.

1940 Federal Census age 24 Marital Status, married to head of house. Lived in Urbana, King, Washington, USA.

1976 Death.

Margaret was married to Erwin Larsen, born about 1910 in Canada English.

They had the following children:

1.   James Larsen, born about 1936 Washington, USA.

1940 Federal Census age 4, living in Urbana, King, Washington, USA.

2.   Larry Larsen born about 1938 Washington, USA.

1940 Census age 2 living in Urbana, King, Washington, USA.

(E.)   GENE L DEACH born July 30, 1919 Washington, USA.

1920 Federal Census age 1 residence Bellingham ward 2, Whatcom, Washington, USA.

1930 Federal Census age 11 residence Marietta, Whatcom, Washington, USA.

1935 age 16 residence Bellingham, Washington, USA.

1940 Federal Census age 20 residence Long Beach, Los Angeles, California, USA marital status married and is the head of house.

September 15 1944 arrived to San Francisco, California, USA.

November 18, 1975 age 56 death, King County, Washington, USA.

Gene married Edna K born 1921. Gene was in the Navy at this time.

Gene was also married to Vivian O'Neil Tucker

(F.)   Ellen J Deach born January 14, 1929 Washington, USA.

1930 Federal Census age 1 resides in Marietta, Whatcom, Washington, USA.

1935 age 6 lives in Marietta, Washington, USA.

1940 Federal Census age 11 resides in Marietta, Whatcom, Washington, USA.

November 3, 1945 age 16 marriage to Robert Giger, Whatcom, Washington, USA.

1948 age 19 residence Bellingham, Washington, USA.

1982 age 53 resided in Edmonds, Washington.

October 16, 1998 death Everett, Washington, USA.

FINLEY MALCOM DEACH

Son of Anges

Born April 10, 1884 Spink, South Dakota, USA.

Death age 61 October 4, 1945 Whidbey Island, Washington, USA. Buried Langley, Island, Washington, USA.

1900 Federal Census age 16 residence Benton & Summer Township, Spink, South Dakota.

1910 Federal Census age 26 residence Beotia, Spink, South Dakota, USA.

October 11, 1911 marriage to Mabel Mae Monte. Spink, South Dakota.

1918 residence Bellingham, Washington, USA.

1940 Federal Census age 56 residence Crescent Island, Washington, USA.

South Dakota Marriages 1905-1989, two citations provide evidence for name, birth, and marriage, residence.

U.S. Directories 1821-1989 two citations provide evidence for name and residence.

U.S. World War 1 Draft Registration Cards, 1917-1918. One citation provided evidence for name, birth, residence.

U.S. World War II Draft Registration Cards, 1942, provides evidence for name, birth and residence.

Washington Death Index, 1940-1996. One citation provides evidence for name, birth and death.

Wife Mabel Mae Monte's parents were Walter C. Monte 1867-1929 and Susan Mae Schalfgen 1868-unknown. Their marriage took place in Caledonia, Racine, Wisconsin, USA. June 9, 1885. Very little has been found on this couple. It has been told that Mabel's mother may be an Indian princess from the Chippewa tribe. According to Merle Deach', DNA great grandson of Walter, there is 14% of his DNA that is unknown.

Mabel was born June 25, 1886 according to her death certificate. Death age 57 Whidbey, Island, Washington, USA. Her first marriage was to Andrew J Bersch. They had two children together.

Walter John Bersch born March 30, 1905, died September 1935 Spokane Washington, USA.

Ardella Willmina Bersch Hardenbrook Landrum born January 19, 1908 Minneapolis Minnesota. Died in 1993. She had one daughter, Vivian Deloris Hardenbrook born June 18, 1925 Bellingham, Washington, USA. She married Jim Baily.

Finley and Mabel had the following children:

(A.) WILBER VERON DEACH "Bill" born January 25, 1913 South Dakota. Died December 24, 1986.

1935 age 22 residence Grandview, Washington, USA.

1940 Federal Census age 27 residence Crescent Island, Washington, USA.

January 25, 1968 age 55, marriage to Marjean E Conkey Snohomish, Washington, USA.

December 24 1986 age 73 death. Burial Lake Forest Park, King County, Washington, USA.

Washington, Marriage Records, 1865-2004 one citation provides evidence for name and marriage.

U.S. Social Security Death Index, 1935-2014, one citation provides evidence for name, birth and death.

(B.) HAZEL MAE DEACH "Dash" born March 6, 1915 Grayling, Atkins, Minnesota, USA.

Died age 85 February 6, 2001, Monroe, Snohomish, Washington, USA.

November 19, 1932, age 17 marriage to Arthur Roper Land, Benton, Washington, USA.

Arthur Roper Land, "Art" born about 1914 Austin, Travis, Texas, USA.

1935 age 20 Hazel resided in Coalfield, King, Washington, USA.

1940 Census age 25, she was married to head of house, lived in Coalfield, King, Washington, USA.

1993 she resided in Seattle, Washington, USA.

February 2, 2001 death age 85 Monroe, Snohomish, Washington, USA.

She was married a second time to Thomas Hawkins, born 1914 died February 20, 1978.

Washington, Marriage Records, 1865-2004, one citation provides evidence for name and marriage to Arthur Land.

Hazel and Arthur had the following children:

1.   Beverly Mae Land born in Grandview, Yakima, Washington, USA.
2.   Eugene Arthur born August 28, 1935 Prosser, Benton, Washington, USA.

1940 Federal Census, Eugene age 4 lived in Coalfield, King, Washington, USA.

October 31, 1957 age 22, married Mattie Ruth Borders in Austin Texas, USA. Her parent's names are Sterling Clyde Borders and Eula Needham.

Eugene and Mattie had the following children:

a.   Carol Sue Land Scifer Robinson born June 13, 1955 Austin, Texas, USA.
b.   Ramona Joyce Land Quesinberry born June 13, 1955 Austin, Texas, USA.
c.   Charles Eugene Land born May 10, 1968 Austin, Texas, USA.

3.   Glen Land born August 28, 1935 Washington, USA.

1940 Federal Census, Eugene age 4 residence Coalfield, King, Washington, USA.

Hazel and Tom had the following children:

1.   Warren Thomas "Sunny" Hawkins born July 1, 1941 Yakima, Washington, USA. Stepson.

Died 2002 buried in Snohomish, Washington, USA.

2.   Sandra Ellen Hawkins born June 21, 1943 Tacoma, Washington, USA. Stepdaughter.

(C.)   THOMAS ROBERT DEACH born April 27, 1917 Enderline, South Dakota, USA.

Died age 78 February 14, 1996 Davenport, Lincoln, Washington, USA.

1935 age 18, he resided in Davenport, Washington, USA.

August 10, 1946 he married Betty Lucile Reed, King, Washington, USA.

U.S. Public Record Index, Volume 2 one citation provides evidence for name, birth and residence.

U.S. Social Security Death Index, 1935-2014, one citation provides evidence for name, birth and death.

Washington Death Index, 1940-1996, one citation provides evidence for name, birth and death.

Washington Marriage Records 1865-2004, one citation provides for name and marriage.

Thomas and Betty had the following children:

1.   Joanne Deach born September 1, 1945.
2.   John Deach born 1945

3.   Thomas Robert Deach born 1947 Renton, Washington, USA.

(D.) ALFRED MONTE DEACH "FRITZ" born February 24, 1919 Bellingham, Washington, USA.

Died age 53 January 20, 1973 Enumclaw Washington, USA.

Burial Greenwood Cemetery Renton Washington, USA.

First marriage to Goldie Darnet Tukamon. This marriage produced one child named Billy Dee. Born about 1940. No information can be found on this person.

Second marriage to Dorothy Helen Dahm Phillips. Born March 9, 1927 New Castle Washington, USA. This was Dorothy's second marriage. She came with two sons. Thomas Marion Dahm and Jack Phillips. She died January 23, 2006 Auburn, Washington, USA. Burial Greenwood Cemetery, Renton Washington, USA. Buried next to third husband Melvin Hjellum. Dorothy had another son Bobby (Robert) who passed away before meeting Alfred. Alfred also had three daughters born somewhere between Goldie and Dorothy. They were adopted out after that relationship ended.

1935 Alfred age 16 living in Grandview Washington, USA.

1940 Federal Census age 21 living in Crescent, Island, Washington, USA.

U.S. World War II Army Enlistment Records, 1938-1946. One citation provides evidence for name, birth and residence.

Washington Death Index, 1940-1996. One citation provides evidence for name, death and residence.

Alfred and Dorothy had the following children:

1. Allen Monte Deach, born April 1, 1949, Washington, USA. Died September 1, 2011. Seattle, King, Washington, USA. Allen had served time in the Viet Nam War he never married.
2. Merle Douglas Deach born April 26, 1950 Prosser Washington. Married Patricia Ann Beall (Robin) June 27, 1970, Kent Washington. They had the following Children:

a. Merle Douglas Deach Jr. born October 24, 1970, Auburn Washington, USA.

Married Jodi Jennifer Mc Cullar, March 20, 1993 Enumclaw Washington, USA.

Jr. married a second time to Linda Foulger.

b. Carlton Monte Deach born October 2, 1973 Auburn, Washington, USA.
c. Jeremy David Deach born October 27, 1980, Renton, Washington, USA.

3. Gary Wayne Deach born May 7, 1951. Died December 26, 2010 Enumclaw Washington, USA.
4. Marshall Deach born June 14, 1952 Washington, USA. Married Debbie last name unknown. They had the following children:

a. Cassie Maria Deach born March 18, 1982, Oregon USA.
b. Allan Dean Deach born August 13, 1986 Oregon, USA.

5. Sharon Lynn Deach born 1953 Washington, USA. Sharon Married Duane Alvin Segebartt July 2, 1971. They had the following children:

a. Christina Lynn Segebartt born March 2, 1975 Washington, USA.
b. Carla Dorothy Segebartt born August 4, 1976 Washington, USA.

6. Carl Malcom Deach born June 1954 Prosser Washington, USA. Died April 28, 1955 Prosser Washington, USA.
7. Sherman Royal Deach born May 1, 1961 Washington, USA. Sherman married Deborah Darlene Miller May 2, 1987. They had the following children:

a. Kassandra Lynn Deach Miller. Born February 1, 1988 Washington, USA.
b. Jebidiah Royal Deach born February 12, 1990, Washington, USA.

(E.) MAXINE MARCELLA DEACH born October 30, 1921 Bellingham, Whatcom, Washington, USA. Death April 2, 1988 age 66, Seattle, King, Washington, USA. Marriage to George Allan Baird, November 18, 1937 in Pasco North, Franklin, Washington, USA. George Allan Baird born March 20, 1919 Dubois, Clark, Idaho, USA. Died February 13 2004 age 84. His parents were Emmett Baird and Minnie Simpson. Maxine and Allan had the following children:

1. Larry Lyn Baird born March 6, 1938 Grandview, Washington, USA. Larry married Alice B Terrill. Her parent were James P Terrill and Hetty E Choyce. Larry and Alice had the following children:

a. Elizabeth M Baird born October 10, 1958 Sunnyside, Washington, USA.
b. Bret A Baird born June 23, 1961 Coos Bay, Oregon, USA.

2. Marlene Baird born July 6, 1941 Oak Harbor, Island, Washington, USA. She married Ted H. Bianchi, August 1, 1958 Coeur d' Alene, Idaho. His parents names Delph Bianchi and Ann Smith. Marlene and Ted had the following children:

a. Teddi Ann Bianchi born November 14, 1958 Prosser, Washington, USA.
b. Terri Alane Bianchi born June 18, 1961 Seattle, Washington, USA.

c. Tammi Alisa Bianchi born June 13, 1963 Seattle, Washington, USA.

3. Kimberly Baird born March 6, 1961 Seattle, Washington, USA. She married Jose C Crist they had the following children:

1. Jose Christopher Crist born 1978.

This marriage ended, she also had the following children:

2. Jarred Loren Baird born 1981.
3. Jolie Allyn Baird born 1983.

(F.) JOHN ANGUS DEACH born September 14, 1925 Bellingham, Whatcom, Washington, USA. Death age 84 July 31, 2010 Centralia, Lewis, Washington, USA. Married Louise Doris Patenaude Centralia, Lewis, Washington, October 3, 1948, First Christian Church Centralia Washington, USA. She was born March 29, 1924. Death November 6, 2003 Centralia, Lewis, Washington USA.

Her parents were James Leonard Patenaude and Marie M Gayewski. John and Louise had the following children:

1. John A Deach born January 10, 1952 Chehalis, Washington, USA.
2. James Finley Deach born April 17 Chehalis, Washington, USA.
3. Larry Lee Deach born September 24, 1956.

G RUTH MARION DEACH born August 12, 1929 Milwaukee, Wisconsin, USA. Death March 7, 2000. First spouse was George Dismuke married April 12, 1950. Second husband Calvin C Tresser married May 28, 1971. Ruth had the following children:

Lonnett Dyann Deach born August 25, 1946 Spokane Washington.

MELINDA ELIZABETH DEACH

Daughter of Anges

Born October 8, 1886 South Dakota.

Death April 13, 1937 age 51 Laurel Heights, Snohomish, Washington, USA. Burial Marysville, Snohomish, Washington, USA.

Melinda married Ivan Rochelle Winters, December 9, 1907 Bellingham, Washington, USA. His parents were Alonzo Clark Winters 1859-1930 and Hannah "Luella" Gracy 1864-1909.

Federal Census 1900 age 14 resided in Detroit Village, Becker, Minnesota.

 Federal Census 1910 age 24 Residence Bellingham married to head of house, residing in Bellingham Ward 1, Whatcom, Washington, USA.

1911 age 25 Residence Bellingham, Washington, USA.

1920 Federal Census age 34 Residence Fords Prairie, Lewis, Washington, USA.

1930 Federal Census age 44 Residence Laurel Heights, Snohomish, Washington, USA.

Melinda and Ivan had the following children:

1. Gertrude Penella Winters born 1905.
2. Gedorne E Winters born 1906 Washington.
3. Baby Winters born 1909 Washington, Died 1909.
4. Velda Winters born June 21, 1910 Washington, USA. Died February 8, 1985 age 74 Cincinnati, Madison, Ohio, USA.

1920 Federal Census, Velda age 10 resides in Fords Prairie, Lewis, Washington, USA.

1930 Federal Census age 20 resides in Laurel Heights, Snohomish, Washington, USA.

Ohio Death Index 1908-1932, 1938-2014 one citation provides evidence for name, birth and death.

Washington, Births, 1883-1935 one citation provides evidence for name and birth.

Velda's spouse was a gentleman with the last name of Laudry.

5. Alonzo Debs "Dee" Winters born November 25, 1910 Aberdeen, Grays Harbor, Washington, USA.

Death December 9, 2006 Stayton, Marion, Oregon, USA. Age 96.

1920 Federal Census age 10 resides in Fords Prairie, Lewis, Washington.

1930 Federal Census age 20 Residence Laurel Heights, Snohomish, Washington, USA.

1935 age 25 resides in Washington, USA.

1940 Federal Census age 29. Residence Stanwood, Snohomish, Washington, USA. Brother to head of house.

July 19 1941 age 30 marriage to Shirley Clare Martin Skagit, Washington, USA.

May 10, 1953 marriage to Dorothy Louise Thompson in Del Norte, California, USA.

U.S. Social Security Death Index 1935-2014, one citation provides evidence for name, death and birth.

6.   Tressa Marie Winters born August 23, 1913, Bellingham, Whatcom, Washington, USA. Death October 20, 2001 age 88 Monroe, Snohomish, Washington, USA.

1920 Federal Census age 7 residence Fords Prairie, Lewis, Washington, USA.

1930 Federal Census age 17 resides in Laurel Heights, Snohomish, Washington, USA.

1935 age 22 resides in Marysville, Washington, USA.

1940 Federal Census age 26 residence Everett, Snohomish, Washington, USA.

1958 Age 45 resides in Seattle, Washington, USA.

Tressa Marie was married to Elbert Davis.

Elbert was born about 1906 King County, Washington, USA.

1910 Federal Census Age 4 resides Seattle Ward 2, King, Washington, USA.

1920 Federal Census age 14 resides East Everett, Washington, USA.

1935 age 29 resides Everett, Washington, USA.

1940 Federal Census age 34 resides in Everett, Washington, USA. Married and is head of house.

1958 age 52 resides in Seattle, Washington, USA.

Tressa and Elbert had the following children:

a. Nancy Davis born about 1938 Washington, USA.

1940 Census age two resides in Everett Washington, USA.

ELIZABETH (BESSIE) MAE DEACH

Daughter of Anges

Born about 1892 South Dakota

1900 Federal Census age 8 Residence Detroit Village, Becker, Minnesota.

1910 Federal Census age 18 Residence Licking, Whatcom, Washington, USA. Relationship to head of house, Stepdaughter.

May 24, 1911 age 19, marriage to George Mitchell, Whatcom Washington, USA. George Mitchell's parents were James Mitchell 1850 and Susanna 1852. George was born about 1884 Wisconsin, USA. In 1900 age 20, he resided in Sun Prairie, Dane, Wisconsin, USA.

1920 Federal Census age 28 resides in Dietrich, Lincoln, Idaho, USA.

1930 Federal Census age 38 resides in Cleveland, Chippewa, Wisconsin, USA. Age 38 married to head of house.

1935 age 43 residence Cornell, Chippewa, Wisconsin. USA.

1940 Federal Census age 48 Residence Cornell Chippewa, Wisconsin, USA.

Washington Marriage Records, 1865-2004 on citation provides evidence for name and marriage. Could find no children to this union.

Theresa- Bess- Linda are the only daughters mention in the Family Recorder.

Death Certificate Angus Deach

Anges Deach taken June 10,1901
Donated by Kathe Deach

Anges Deach

Thomas Deach taken 1905
Donated by Kathe Deach

Finley on left and Jim Deach

Finley and Mabel Deach about 1938

Beth- Theresa-Melinda Deach

Wilber- Tom- Alfred- John- Ardella- Hazel- Maxine- Ruth Deach

JOHN W DEACH

BROTHER OF ANGES DEACH

JOHN WILLIAM DEACH

October 23, 1845-April 17, 1916
Son of AUGUST DEACH and MARTHA SCHULTZ

Born October 23, 1845 Germany.

1860 age 15 entered into the United States.

1870 Federal Census age 25 residence Cass, Clayton, Iowa, USA.

1871 age 26 marriage to Lucinda Reed.

1880 Federal Census age 35 residence Portland, Cerro Gordo, Iowa, USA.

1888 July 25th age 42 resided in Spink, South Dakota, USA.

1900 Federal Census age 55 residence Rock Grove, Floyd, Iowa, USA.

1910 Federal Census age 65 residence Charles City, Iowa, USA.

1915 age 70 resided in Nora Springs, Floyd, Iowa, USA.

April 17, 1916 age 70 death, Nora Springs, Iowa.

Iowa, Cemetery Records, 1662-1999 one citation provides evidence for name, birth and death.

Sarah Lucinda Reed, born January 18, 1846 Polk, Crawford, Ohio, USA.

1850 Federal Census age 4 residence Polk, Crawford, Ohio, USA.

February 28, 1916 age 70 death- Bramer, Missouri, USA. Buried next to her husband John, at Park Cemetery, Nora Springs, Iowa, USA.

Iowa Cemetery Records one citation provides evidence for name, birth and death.

Obituary announcement in local newspaper Mrs. J. W. Deach, an old and highly respected citizen of Nora Springs, died at the home of her daughter in Braymer, Mo., last Monday, and the body was brought to Nora Springs Wednesday morning. The funeral will take place from the M.E. church today (Thursday) at 2:30. Owing to our going to press early, we will be deferred from publishing the obituary until next week.

Mrs. J. W. Deach Sarah Lucinda Reed was born in Ohio, January 18, 1847. When a child her parents moved to Cerro Gordo County, Iowa, where she grew to womanhood. In 1871, she was united in marriage to J. W. Deach. They lived for a few years on a farm west of Nora Springs, and they moved with their family to South Dakota. After a few years they came back to Iowa and have lived in Nora Springs until last fall when they went to live with their daughter Mrs. Frank Wetzel, at Braymer, Mo., where she lived until February 28, 1916, when after an illness of two weeks she passed away. She leaves to mourn her loss, her husband and six children, Elmer Deach of Glyndon, Minn., Clara Wetzel, of Braymer, Mo., Lillian Mathers, of Nora

Springs, Grace Riley, of Lincoln, Neb., John Deach and Anna Deach both of Nora Springs. She also has a brother L. W. Reed, of Rockford Iowa, and a sister Mrs. O. B. Roberts, of Denver Colorado. Early in life, she united with the primitive Baptist church and has since been a true consistent Christian woman. Mrs. Deach was a devoted wife and mother and a friend whom to know was to love.

August 25, 2014 the reaper, Death has gathered many from the community of Nora Springs this winter. Since the death of Mrs. John Deach Sr., a count of the number of funeral services that have taken place here shows that seven have been buried in Park Cemetery and five on Rock Grove Cemetery, one in the Reed Cemetery and one in a cemetery further north of town. Mrs. Deach's burial will be the fifteenth; all of the deaths have been caused by lingering diseases particulars of whose death is given by our Plymouth correspondent died at the home of her daughter Mrs. Frank Wetzel a 4 o'clock Monday morning. She was 69 years one month and nine days of age-having been born in Ohio Jan. 18, 1847. She has been in poor health for some months two of her sons were to see her during the winter. Her demise was not a surprise. The remains were taken to Nora Springs, Iowa, the family home burial accompanied by her husband and Mr. and Mrs. Frank Wetzel.

Cards of Thanks We wish to thank our old friends and neighbors for their many kindnesses and favors that were shown us during our late bereavement and for the many beautiful floral offerings. Elmer Deach. Mrs. Clara Wetzel, Mrs. W. S. Mathers, Mrs. Grace Riley, John B. Deach, Miss Anna Deach.

Cards of Thanks; To the friends and neighbors who have given and kindly assistance, sympathy and beautiful flowers during our recent bereavement we wish to extend our heartfelt thanks. J. W. Deach and Family.

The children of John and Lucinda are as follows:

DAVID ELMER DEACH born January 8, 1872, Iowa, USA. Three miles north of Nora Springs per personal letter to his daughter Grace. Died September 29, 1941.

CLARA THERESA DEACH born May 28, 1876 Nora Springs, Floyd, Iowa, USA. Died April 19, 1953 Braymer, Missouri, USA.

GRACE E DEACH born February 3, 1881 Portland, Cerro Gordo, Iowa, USA. Died September 6, 1941 Sheridan Wyoming, USA.

JOHN BYRON DEACH born September 13, 1883 South Dakota, USA. Died August 19, 1948 Clear Lake, Cerro Gordo, Iowa, USA.

R ANNA DEACH born July 25, 1888 Spink, South Dakota, USA. Died August 1970 Basin, Big Horn, Wyoming, US

DAVID ELMER DEACH

Son of John W Deach

Born January 8, 1872 Yaggie Farm, Iowa, three miles north of Nora Springs, USA.

1880 Federal Census age 8 residence Portland, Cerro Gordo, Iowa, USA.

1895 age 23 resided in Nora Springs, Floyd, Iowa, USA.

1896 age 24 marriage to Katherine Ladworoski.

1900 Federal Census age 28 residence Rock Grove, Floyd, Iowa, USA.

1910 Federal Census age 38 residence Owen, Cerro Gordo, Iowa, USA.

1920 Federal Census age 48 residence Glydon, Clay, Minnesota, USA.

1930 Federal Census age 58 residence Garden, Polk, Minnesota, USA.

1940 Federal Census age 68 residence Woodside, Polk, Minnesota, USA.

September 26, 1941 age 69, death.

Burial Terrebonne, Red Lake County, Minnesota, USA.

Katherine Ladworoski born October 25, 1872 Mecan, Marquetta, Wisconsin, USA.

1900 Federal Census age 28 residence Rock Grove, Floyd, Iowa, USA.

1910 Federal Census age 38 residence Owen, Cerro Gordo, Iowa, USA.

1920 Federal Census age 48 residence Glydon Clay, Minnesota, USA.

1930 Federal Census age 58 residence Garden, Polk, Minnesota, USA.

October 28, 1939 age 67 death, Crookston, Polk, Minnesota, USA.

Elmer and Katherine had the following children:

1.   Neve Ruth Deach born October 1897 Iowa, USA.

1900 Federal Census age 3 resided in Rock Grove, Floyd, Iowa, USA.

1910 Federal Census age 13 residence Owen, Cerro Gordo, Iowa, USA.

1920 Federal Census age 23 residence Glydon, Clay, Minnesota, USA.

1935 age 38 resided Rural, Clay, Minnesota, USA.

1940 Federal Census age 42 Residence Highland Grove, Clay, Minnesota, USA.

July 10, 1989 age 91 death, Clay, Minnesota, USA.

Minnesota, Death Index, 1908-2002 one citation provides evidence for name, birth and death.

Neve married James Lebeda, born May 15, 1900 Nebraska, USA.

Parents were Joseph Lebeda born 1856 and wife Fanny born 1861.

Neve and James had the following children:

a.   Kenneth C Lebeda born about 1929 Minnesota.

1935 age six residence Rural, Clay, Minnesota, USA.

1940 Federal Census age 11 residence Highland Grove, Clay, Minnesota, USA.

August 28 1946 age 17 Military

1986 age 57 residence Hitterdal, Minnesota, USA.

February 1, 1993 age 64 death, Hitterdal, Minnesota, USA.

Burial Hitterdal, Clay County, Minnesota, USA.

U.S. Department of Veterans Affairs BIRLS Death File. 1850-2010 one citation provides evidence for name, death, birth, military.

b.   Mary Ann Lebeda born February 1 1935 Clay County, Minnesota, USA.

Death February 1, 1935 Clay County, Minnesota, USA.

2.   Verle E Deach born April 11, 1901 Iowa, USA.

1910 Federal Census age 9 residence Owen, Cerro Gordo, Iowa, USA.

1920 Federal Census age 19 residence Glyndon, Clay, Minnesota, USA.

1935 age 34 resided in Alexandria, Douglas, Minnesota.

1940 Federal Census age 38 residence Minneapolis, Hennepin, Minnesota, USA.

1950 age 49 residence Minneapolis, Minnesota, USA

February 27, 1982 death Hennepin, Minnesota, USA.

Burial Minneapolis, Hennepin County, Minnesota, USA.

Verle married Marvel Francis Nichols born December 29, 1903 North Dakota, USA.

1935 age 32 residence Alexandria, Douglas, Minnesota, USA

1940 Federal Census age 36 residence Minneapolis, Hennepin, Minnesota, USA.

May 1992 death Minneapolis, Hennepin, Minnesota, USA.

U.S. Social Security Death Index, 1935-2014 one citation provides evidence for name, death and birth.

Verle and Marvel had the following children:

a.　George Nichola Deach born May 28, 1934 North Dakota. 1935 age one resided Shakopee, Minnesota, USA.

1940 Federal Census age 5 residence Minneapolis, Hennepin, Minnesota, USA.

1986 age 52 residence Minneapolis, Minnesota, USA.

April 12, 1999 age 64, death.

U.S. Social Security Death Index, 1935-2014 one citation provides evidence for name, death and birth.

Could not find a spouse or child.

b.　David Deach born April 17, 1937 Hennepin, Minnesota, USA.

1940 Federal Census age 2 resides in Minneapolis, Hennepin, Minnesota, USA.

1993 age 56 residence Apple Valley, Minnesota, USA.

Minnesota Birth Index, 1935-2002 one citation provides evidence for name and birth.

Could not find spouse or child.

3.　Grace E Deach born October 26, 1907 Iowa, USA

1910 Federal Census age 3 residence Owen, Cerro Gordo, Iowa, USA.

1920 Federal Census age 13 residence Glyndon, Clay, Minnesota, USA.

September 10, 1928 age 20 marriage to Wesley Barta Hawley, Minnesota, USA.

1935 age 28 residence Parke, Clay Minnesota, USA.

1940 Federal Census age 32 rresidence Parke, Clay, Minnesota, USA.

July 19, 1993 age 85 death Barnesville, Minnesota.

Wesley Barta was born April 2, 1902 Nebraska, USA. His parent were Joseph John Barta 1863-1928 and Sophie Jennie Klimes 1872-1935. Wesley died May 24, 1970 age 68 Crystal Bay, Hennepin County, Minnesota, USA. Grace and Wesley had the following children:

a.   Wesley Barta Jr. born about 1930 Minnesota.

1935 age 6 resided in Parke, Clay, Minnesota, USA.

1940 Federal Census age 11 residence Parke, Clay, Minnesota, USA.

March 12, 2008 age 79 death Barnesville, Clay, Minnesota.

U.S. Social Security Death Index, 1935-2014

One citation provides evidence for name, birth and death.

Could not find spouse or child.

b.   Virgil Barta born March 28, 1929.

1935 age four residence Parke, Clay, Minnesota, USA.

1940 Federal Census age 9 residence Parke, Clay, Minnesota, USA.

June 24 1950 age 19 marriage to Donna Jean Jacobs Washington, Minnesota. Her parents were Nick Jacobs and Enez.

I could find no children for this union.

March 2, 2012 age 82 Virgil died, Minnesota, USA.

May 8, 1979 age 45 Donna died. Burial Blooming, Monroe County, Indiana, USA.

c.   George Barta born about 1933 Minnesota, USA.
d.   Rita Lorraine Barta born April 12, 1935 Hawley, Clay County, Minnesota, USA.

1940 Federal Census, Rita age 4 residence Parke, Clay, Minnesota, USA.

1995 age 60 residence Callaway, Minnesota, USA.

May 2 2009 age 74-death Innovis health, Fargo, Cass County, North Dakota, USA. U.S. Social Security Death Index, 1935-2014 one citation provides evidence for name death and birth.

Rita married Reuben J Jaster who was born July 22, 1933. Died February 20 1994 Callaway, Becker County, Minnesota, USA.

The following information was found on Ancestry regarding Rita Barta.

Rita L Jaster, 74 rural Callaway, died Saturday, May 2, 2009, in Innovis Health in Fargo N. D.

Rita was born on April 12, 1935 to Wesley and Grace (Deach) Barta in Hawley. She had a twin brother that died at birth. Rita attended country school near Rollag and later attended school in Hawley, where she participated in F. H. A. and 4-H. She graduated from Hawley High School in 1953. As a young woman, she worked as a waitress in Fargo, when she met Reuben Jaster. Rita went to New Jersey, where Rueben was station in the military. They were united in marriage on Dec. 21, 1955, in Wheatfield, N.J.

Rita and Reuben moved back to Callaway to take over the operation of Reuben's family farm. They moved to Bloomington for a short time before returning to Callaway. Rita worked at Jim's and Betty's Superette in Callaway, as well as Gambles Hardware Store in Ogema for many years and eventually became the main cook at the Nutrition Center in Callaway for 24 years, until retiring in 2001. Rita always put a 100 percent into her job and touched many with her cooking ability. Rita's favorite job of all was being a full time mother and grandmother to all of her family and extended families. With Rita being such a great cook all of her friends and family would call on Rita to cook for confirmations, graduations and weddings. They all wanted Rota's famous potato salad. Rita's hobbies included many.

She loved making rag rugs long ones and Buggy Wheel rugs. She would demonstrate her hobby up at Rollag during Minnesota Steam Thresher's Reunion as well as Albany Pioneer Days every fall. Rita also loved to paint, crochet, knit, and make baby blankets for all of her extended families, when they would have children.

Rita is survived by two sons, Matthew (Cheng) Jaster, Lake Park, Kyle (Tina) Jaster, Lake Park; three daughters, Leda (Bruce) Franklin, Callaway, DeeAnna Brockway, Callaway, Anita (Bruce) Coons, Eau Claire, Wis,; 11 great grandchildren four great-grandchildren, two brothers, Virgil (Agnes) Barta, Moorehead, George (Evelyn Barta, Bloomington; one sister, Donna Wilson, Grand Forks, and several nieces and nephews.

Rita was preceded in death by her parents, husband, Reuben, two sons, Timothy John and Joseph Reuben; two brothers, Wesley and Loren Barta; one sister, Phyllis Spitka, and a sister-in-law, Ruth Barta. The funeral services is Wednesday, May 6, 2009 at 11a.m. in Immanuel Lutheran Church Callaway.

Visitation is Tuesday, from 4-7 p.m. in Immanuel Lutheran Church, with prayer service at 7 p.m.

Internment is in Oak Grove Cemetery, Detroit Lakes.

West-Kjos Funeral Home, Detroit Lakes, is taking care of arrangements.

e.   Audrey Marciel Deach born June 7 1915 Minnesota.

1920 Federal Census age 5 residence Glyndon, Clay, Minnesota, USA.

1930 Federal Census age 15 residence Garden, Polk, Minnesota, USA.

1940 Federal Census age 24 residence Woodside, Polk, Minnesota, USA.

December 17, 1992 age 77 death, Crookston, Polk County, Minnesota, USA.

Minnesota, Death Index, 1908-2002 one citation provides evidence for name, birth and death.

AUTOBIOGRAPHY OF ELMER D DEACH

February 27, 1936 as written for daughter

I, Michelle Barta Khan, have retyped the photocopy of the typed copy of Elmer's letter to Grace as best I could. Anything that I could not read has been highlighted. I either left it as I saw it, or put in word I believe it to be. Egan, Minnesota June 30, 2010.

I Grace Deach Barta, asked my father one time to write a autobiography. The following is what he wrote. I have the original in his own writing. Mento, Minnesota Feb 27, 1936.

Dear Grace,

I will try and send this tomorrow or the next day. My was that an awful snow yesterday, gosh the snow is over three feet deep in the timber. We got a letter from Neve today. They have to move and are moving on a 400-acre farm 3 miles south of Hitterdahl [Hitterdal]. Well Grace this history is kind of mixed up. There is incidents that I forgot to put at the right place but I tried to make it lain on the margin. If there are, incidents that you think are of no use leave them out. Add such as you wish that happened after you could remember. Write. Lots of love. Let me know what you think of it. Lots of love Dad.

I Elmer Deach, was born on a very cold morning January 8, 1872, three miles north of Nora Springs Iowa on which is known as the Yaggie farm. My parents were John? Deach and Lucindia Reed. They were both 24 years old, being both born in the year 1847. My father was born in Germany and came to Ontario Canada when he was 7 years old with his mother who was a widow, two brothers' (William and Angus) and a sister Mary. He and Mary were bound out to Quaker family by the name of Jacob Stover. His mother married, moved to Michigan and was never to hear of again. Angus and William shifted for themselves. Father stayed with the Stover's until he was 18 years old. He was given $100.00, and a new suit of clothes and he was on his own. He learned that Choose Making Trade and worked at that one year. He and his brother Angus went to Iowa and each bought 120 acres three miles west of Nora Springs. This was in the 1865. His sister Mary married a man named John Brumpton. I never saw any of their large family but Will Brumpton. He lived at Shevlin Minnesota and died in 1917. William, the oldest joined the U.S. Army in 1861 and was never heard from.

Now the ancestors of my mother's family "The Reeds", her father was born in Massachusetts somewhere around 1810. Grandfather was as we say a Genuine Pioneer. As a young man he went to the now state of Maine, took a farm and improved but the call of the west got in his blood. He sold out, moved to Ohio, and improved on another farm. In the mean time, he married a girl Rachel Cumings. They have seven children Lorenzo, Sylvia, Adeline, Sapronia, Lucindia (my mother) Isaac and Elvira. In 1849, when Chicago was only a trading post they moved to Iowa. They settled on a farm one half mile north of the one father settled on later in 1866. Grandfather and the rest were real pioneers. They carded their own wool-spun the thread, wove, and dyed the yarn and cloth. I have seen Grandmother weaving many times. If they had anything to sell, they had to haul it to Debuque [Dubugue] – 175 miles. Then to McGregor and then to Waverly which was only 50 miles. In the 60's the Milwaukee railroad came to Mason City. They were in Iowa when the new Ulm massacre occurred in Minnesota. That was about 50 miles away. Grandmother died in 1877 and her mother, Grandma Cumings died about the same time. She was 99 years old.

Up until 1881, my life was that of any normal boy. I went to school, played, and got into mischief. The only happenings of any importance was the birth of Claira on May 28, 1876, Lillian Nov 20, 1877 and Grace Feb 3, 1881.

At harvest time in 1881, hired help was very scarce and high, 3 dollars a day.

Father had me drive the old Marsh harvester while father and the hired man bound it. I remember one day we were cutting oats and it was awful heavy and the hired man couldn't take care of his share of it as it came down onto the binding platform. Father told him to get off and shock. He bound it alone.

In the spring of 1881. Grandfather went to Spink County S. Dakota; Uncle Isaac took homestead, built a sod house and barn. It was very wet in Iowa that year so father decided to sell out. He went to South Dakota and filed on a homestead cornering Uncle Isaac's on the northwest. Then in the spring of 1882 we went to So. Dakota with the following people. Uncle Angus (married to Malinda Kelly). Uncle Marion Allen (married to Aunt Adeline Reed). Uncle Wilson Allison (married to Saphronia). A Mr. Brown (the father of Mallissa, wife of Uncle Isaac). They all went to Ashton, the end of the Milwaukee railroad. South of Aberdeen and then to Huron So. Dakota.

Then we all went to Uncle Isaac's. When night came, there was not room for all of us to sleep in the house so the rest of us had to hit the hay in the barn. Every inch of floor space in the house was covered in bedding. When one got up, they had to step over someone else. Then with a loan of most essentials things, we moved into our own 16 by 16 shack. I went with father to (Ashton 20 miles) after a load of our belongings and I never saw so much stuff as there was along that siding. It was anyway a mile long and the prairie was absolutely covered the whole length with crates, boxes etc.

In May, we children with hired man (Alonzo Boulty) got the measles and we were all down at once. Mother sure had her hands full. As early as they could, father started the hired man to break the virgin sod. Just a few acre's of oats and wheat but we had a wonderful garden. Father broke 100 acres of sod then broke a lot for others for $5.00 an acre. That summer father build a new 16x24, 1-1/2 story house of rough boards on the outside and then sod it up to the upstairs. The lower floor was mine and warm but the upstairs was sure cold. When it was 45 or 50 degrees below, you could hear the nails pull and frost inches thick all over the walls. But next summer we had to move. Father had filed on a tree claim 2 miles northeast of the homestead. He had dug a lot of wells but could not find enough water to supply us on. The tree claim he succeeded in making a good well at about 20 feet.

Brother John was born in 1883. We children did not get to go to school until that year. They built a schoolhouse just ½ mile west of our house. In the spring of 1883, a lot more people came out from Iowa. Uncle Lorenzo Reed. Smith follows and his two sons, Barthilemire and pierce. Smith Fellows wife was a sister to Grandfather Reed. Orlando Roberts came out and married Elvira Reed.

In the fall of 82, I was set to work on the farm. Father bought a Gelpin 2 wheel self-lifting sulky plow. It took three horses I backed all they had broke that summer. When I started to work in the field, I got my first coffee to drink. Us children were never allowed tea or coffee until we were old enough to work.

The next year father put in a lot of wheat. He purchased a new McCormick self- binder but he did not get the bundle carrier for it cost $5.00 more. My job was to carry the bundle together and the hired man shocked them.

For amusement in the winter, we had literary society in the schoolhouse and dances in the houses of the neighbors. I started to dance the winter of 83 and still do, once in a while. I am now 64 as I write this.

In 1885, we had a good crop of wheat and that winter father, mother, Grace, and John went to Canada to see his sister Mary. Grandfather Reed died and was buried on Uncle Isaac's tree claim. Mr. Brown was also buried there. Mr. Brown died about a week after he arrived from Iowa. Aunt Adeline died of heart one night. She was also buried there. They all moved to Turton when we left So. Dakota in 1891.

I think it was in 1867 they put a railroad from Doland to Groton and Turton, which was 4-1/2 miles due east. Just after we moved out there, there was a railroad put through from Water town to Redfield and Doland, which was 15 miles S.E. of us. Ashton was 22 miles west of us. Doland was our trading post until the railroad came to Turton.

Father was a great man to hunt and was a wonderful shot both with the shotgun and rifle. In the spring of 81, two antelopes went through our place. Father and the hired man hitched up a team of beautiful bay geldings (father sold them 2 years later for $400.00), took after them, and caught up with them 5 miles west of us in what was known as dry run. It was very rough there and father sneaked up close enough to shoot and kill one of them. That winter there was a herd of 9 or 10 antelope about

10 miles N.E. of us in the Big Slew. It was the head of Timber Creek. Father and some neighbors went up there every day to try and [get] them. One day the rest of the men drove some right past the haystack they was hiding behind and he shot a big buck. That same winter he shot a long one about three miles west of our place. Then one time they found some in a draw, this time, I went along. They took a team, and drove through the long draw and chased them up towards father. Boy was I excited. I was there when that antelope started away from us. She look just like a big snowball bouncing away. The big buck father shot he tanned. What a job he could do. The hide side was as white as snow and soft as any buckskin you ever saw. He also tanned fox and wolf hides. He sold them all to a civil engineer that was running a survey for railroad through our land and they camped at our place. I forgot what he was paid for the skins but it seemed like a big price at the time. I went with father twice for wolves. The first one was 3 miles west of where we lived. He had been seen over there often. Father set a trap for him. He built a small sod place, put a dead small pig in it, and set his trap in the entrance. The next morning a neighbor came over and said that the wolf had pawed the trap and turned it upside down, taken the pig. We drove over and followed his tracks in the snow, we found him a mile south, and we drove to the east of him. He wanted to go east to Timber Creek where it was kind of rough. He started to go north and the farther he went the faster he went. The faster he went the faster we went. The farther we went the closer we were coming together until we were not more than 3 or 4 rods apart. We were coming to a place of breaking that was 10 or 15 rods side. Just before we got to it father said slow up so I can jump. He jumped but kept his footing. When the sled hit the plowing, it made an awful noise. The wolf slowed up, looked around, and saw father. The wolf crumbled like a bubble. The bullet went right through him and came out his mouth.

That spring Uncle Angus came over and said there was a wolf at the N.W. corner of our land. Someone had hauled a dead horse out there. Uncle Angus had his team and good sleighing. It was 6 miles up there and the wolf started off to the north. He only went a little way and hid behind a thick bunch of woods. We drove as if to go by, then we got even, Father said to stop. As soon as we stopped, the wolf started straight away. Father shot and you should have seen that wolf turn summersaults. End over end then he got onto his feet and away he went. Uncle Angus took after him as fast as his team would go. We followed him 2 miles. We could see by the blood in the snow that he was badly hurt. After a while, he just became so weak he laid down.

In those days, there were thousands of prairie chickens and White Brants. Just thousands of them went through every spring and fall. One spring morning they began to come from the South and commenced to light just ½ mile from home. They kept coming for 2 or 3 hours. The whole section seemed just white as if it had snowed. I had an old zoolo britch-loading shotgun with brass shells. I only had six shells and they did not last long.

One time I, Mitchel, Joshua and Filep (they had a single barrel muzzle loading shot gun) went hunting prairie chickens. We had very little shot and the chickens were plentiful so we were soon out of shot. We went down to the house and got popcorn. We got all the chickens that we wanted.

I finished common school in 86 or 87. The teacher (Ella Engler) wanted me to go and take examinations and teach but I would not do so.

On 12 January 1888 was the awful blizzard. One of the worst that was ever known up to that time. Lots of people froze to death. Thousands of cattle too. We were in school and stayed all night. It was so sudden. Just a clap of thunder and you could not see. In the morning, before we were playing with snowballs and the next morning it was 40 degrees below zero.

About this time father went into dairy and he built up a herd of 20 cows. He started a little cheese factory. The cheese was sold at the towns of Redfield, Aston, Malletts, Aberdsen, Croton, Turton, Doland, and Frankfort. He had a 3 seated spring buggy and a span of ponies' He would load up 800 to 1000 lbs of cheese and start the rounds. Aberdeen was 40 miles away and he would sometimes be back by 4 in the afternoon.

Before I forget, when we arrived in So. Dakota the county seat was at Old Ashton about half ways between Ashton and Redfield on the James River. The railroad had just came into that county in 80 or 81. In the spring of 83, the word came over the grape vine that Redfield had sold the county seat. The next day I think every man in the county went to Redfield and besieged the town. Every man had a gun. There were guns of every date and vintage. There's enough levelheaded men to ward off a clash, which really would have happened if just one shot had been fired. It was settled by letting the records be taken to Ashton. They had an election the next fall. Ashton went ahead, bonded the town for 10,000 dollars, and built a county court house on the strength of winning the election. Redfield won the election that fall and Ashton had a courthouse but ne court.

When we first went to So. Dakota there was no Buffalo. Once in a while, we would hear of one being killed near Mallet. The older settlers said that in 83 there were lots of them until the Indians turned the county over to the government. During the winter, the Indians made a big drive and drove all the Buffalo over the Missouri River. When the river was frozen over there were lots of, Buffalo on the west side of the river and Buffalo robes were very cheap. $5.00 to $10.00 a piece. Coats for about $20.00.

In 88, Uncle Lorenzo Reed sold his place to Mr. Lapham and moved back to Iowa. Uncle Orlando Roberts went the same time. In the mean time, Father had built a new barn 32x30 with haymen. We had many dances. We thought nothing of driving 12 to 15 miles in the winter to a dance. In the summer time sometimes 30 miles.

In the fall of 1890 Father and Mother made up their minds to get out of So. Dakota. The crops seemed to be getting very poor. In the spring of 91 father hired out to make choose at Leileys Lake at $100.00 a month. Before this in the winter, he went down into Tennessee and decided to move there in the fall. When father went to work that left us to put in crops. The crops has been sold during the winter or given away for $20, a piece.

In 1890, they organized a band in Turton, I joined and played E flat alto Clarinet. Our band played at the Aberdeen State Fair. We boosted for Aberdeen. At that time there was a three cornered fight between Huron, Pierre and Aberdeen for the Capital of So. Dakota, Pierre won at the election that fall.

In the spring of 1883-, one Sunday morning dad said lets go fishing. Where? To Clyde's Mill. It was 12 miles west on the Jim River, where the river is in the shape of a big----. We got over there about eleven o'clock. The dam was made by cutting trees, brush 12 to 15 feet long, laying them down, and putting dirt on them. A spillway in the center about 20 feet long. In the building the dam they made the first layer very wide but only about a foot high. The next foot layer was a foot narrower. So on the north side it made steps. I am giving this description for another fish story. When we got to the dam there must have been a couple hundred people there. And were they ever catching fish. You could see a dozen fish in the air all the time. We had to go to the bottom of the line. Father cut a couple of short—illions poles. Put on a piece of muskrat steak and we threw it in and inside of two minutes we were hauling out 2 to

5 lbs Pickerel. We were not there more than three-quarters of an hour and we had 36. Just all father and I could carry down to the buggy. That was the best fishing I ever had.

I think it was the next year that father was going to Ashton and he went by Clyde's Mill. Josh, Mitchel Phillip, and Smith Reed went with us. Us four stopped to fish while father went into Ashton. There was nothing there but black suckers. There were a lot of people there fishing but the suckers wouldn't bite. We put big hooks on our lines and a heavy rock to sink the hook to the bottom. Then we gave it a quick jerk. The fish were so thick that we caught many of that day. But that was slow for me. I rolled up my pant legs and sleeves, knelt down on the lowest step of the dam and put my hand down into the water. The fish were so thick they were touching one another. I just felt around until I got my fingers under their gills and then throw them up to the boys on top of the dam. In a little while we had three sacks full. Then father came and off for home.

It's now fall of 1891 and we make preparations to go to Tennessee. All the cattle, machinery, and horses except eight. One wagon and a three seated spring buggy. These we put covers on and the latter part of September, we pulled out for Tennessee. The other horses were 1 span of 1 year old filly's and one two year old gelding and one 3 year old. Those were tied behind the covered rigs and what a time I had with the two geldings. They were big brutes and would not lead. I had to just about drag them. When we started up a hill, they could stop the wagon. Father had stayed behind to finish the business and was to meet us in Mason City Iowa. Along with us was another family. John Paxton. They had quite a family, five children. I remember the little boy; he was about a year and a half old. Boy he could cry. When we stopped at night, he would just bawl and bawl, until he cried himself to sleep. We were all disgusted with him and it was the same every night until they left us at Fairmont Minn. They went south to Boone Iowa. ---went south east across country all the way. There is a little incident that happen while the Paxton's were with us. Mr. Paxton had a span of gray mares; one of them was blind and very slow. He also had a suckling colt and he traded the blind mare and the colt for a brown gelding. We started out and the first hill we came to it stopped. So we fooled with that pesky horse for an hour but we could not make him move. We tried everything and at last, I remember something I had heard. It was worth a try at least. We tied his tail to the single tree and away we. But it was the same thing every time we came to a sizable hill.

The first night we camped across state line in Gray Minn. I had been having such a time with the colts that I told mother that I was going to sell them the first chance I got. There was just too much work taking care of eight horses. We drove into Marshall there was a crowd collected around a couple of cattle and horse buyers. In a little while I had sold them for $300.00. – To Tracy Minn. And we made camp for the weekend. We had been making 40 miles a day. Monday we went south to Windom and then to Fairmont. Here the Paxton's left us. This was one of the prettiest towns that we saw on our whole trip. Just on, the south edge of town is a nice lake and we camped on the bank. East to Blue Earth and south to the Iowa state line. That night we met the meanest man on our whole trip. It was pretty cold that day, the wind from the North West. This man's house was in Minn. And his barn in Iowa, around his house on three sides was a fine grove of trees. I stopped and asked the man if I could water the horses and camp out of the wind. NO drive on and don't camp around here. The horses were tired so no just drove about 80 rods down the road and camped in a hay field. The horses had plenty of hay but no water. Next day we went through Coon Grove. Just after noon, it started to drizzle and kept it up for the rest of the day. We got to Forest City about 4 o'clock went south from there looking for a place to stay. At last, we came to a farm with a big barn. I wanted to get the horses in side if possible. I went in and asked them. They were an old couple and they said drive your wagons right in on our barn floor. Tie the horses in the stalls. We done so and then they had us come into the house to get warm. They made us coffee. We sleep in the barn on the hay. The morning was clear and a dandy day. We got to Mason City around noon. Father was here to meet us. In the afternoon we went down to Uncle Lorenzo's. We stayed in Iowa 2 weeks visiting all of the relations. Then off for Tennessee.

We went south through Hockford, Waverly, Waterloo, Cedar Rapids, Iowa City to Muscatine. We had intended to take a boat from there but it would be two or three days till a boat would come so we decided to drive to Dubuque. That was 20 miles farther but we were there that evening. Just after we left Muscatine, I saw a tree with some attractive fruit on it. I asked father what kind of fruit it was. He said Persimmons. I got off the wagon and filled my hat. They tasted real good. In a few minutes, our mothers were puckered up so we looked like kids trying to whistle, of course, it soon wore off. If you wait until after frost, they are delicious and do not have a puckering, affect. We stopped and camped for a day. Just after dinner, we saw a team coming down the road. An old man driving and we got to where we were there was an old woman sitting in the bottom of the box. They were both drunk. They stopped and the old man got out a quart of whiskey and nothing would do but we all drank with them. After a while, they drove down the road singing and apparently very happy. We hitched up, drove into Burlington, and stayed down by the river for two days, until the boat came. They loaded us on the boat and away we went for St. Louis. There we were to change boats.

The trip down the Mississippi was grand. What an experience at Keokuk Iowa. They put us through the rapids, through a canal and locks. It was a grand sight to see them roustabouts (colored slaves) load and unload goods. The first mate stood up on the upper deck and the second mate stood out on the gangplank.

He had a hickory cane and if a niger did not move fast enough down would come the cane across his back. Did he move then. Once in a while one of them would hide somewhere in the cargo to get out of helping unload. Somebody was sure to miss him and they would begin to look for him. What they done to them was something else again. The only time I was off the boat was at Hannabel Mo. It was very nice town. Sometime during the second night, we got to St. Louis. Got up in the morning and went ashore to find a place to put our horses. Stayed two days, our wagons were just in under the old Eadox Bridge. It was one of the largest bridges of that time. Two days wait and onto another boat. This time we are headed for Carla, then we go to the mouth of the Ohio River they piled up to the bank and put us off on a sand bar on the Kentucky side. We camped here on the sandbar in a grove of Hickory and Beech trees. Now we are on the last lap headed for Greenfield Tenn.

That night we camped at a farm. Along about 8 o'clock a boy and two girls came down to camp and asked if I would go to a dance with them. I've been sorry ever since that, I did not go. Too bashful, I think. Two or three days after we got to Greenfield Tenn., a small town 10 miles south of Memphis. We stayed with some people by the name of H.H. Hillix. They had two daughters. Moolie and Lockie. The first night they had a bunch of their friends meet us. We had a grand time. Then father was taken sick and got no better, we stayed only 10 days and they make up their minds to go to Iowa. Father sold one of the teams. Father and Mother and the rest of the family, went back on the train. I stayed behind to deliver the team and load the rest of our belongings into a freight car. It left Friday morning and got into Mason City Monday night. Father met me. He stayed that night and took a load of stuff out to Uncle Landies at Ruff. We went back next day and rented the Jack Norse farm 6 miles east of Nora Springs. That was the fall of 92.

The spring of 93, I was 21 years old. I went back to So. Dakota and worked for Van Morman at $26.00 a month. Stayed until fall and got sick so I went back to Iowa. That was the year of the World's Fair in Chicago. I had intended to go but for some reason I did not.

Father had bought a Restaurant and Hotel in Nora Springs.

In the fall of 94, I got hold of a span of horses and got a job hauling cream to Rock Falls, 7 or 8 miles n.e. of Nora Springs. $2.00 a day and sure was glad to get it. Feb 10, 1896 I married Katherine Ladworoski. In the fall the panic. The banks closed, the creamery closed, and I was out of a job. There was just no work of any kind from Nov until next August. I tell you it was very hard pickings. I do not think I earned $25.00 all those months. Neve was born on Oct 20, 1897.

In August, I got a job as a roustabout in a butcher shop and worked there until just before Xmas. In January a fellow by the name of Tom Gear and I went to cut cut wood for old John Whitsel, south of town. We had only worked 3 days when a tree fell on me and nearly killed me. I was layed up for a month. I had walked under a tree lodged in another the 3 days we were working. Somehow, this tree had shifted during the night and when I walked under it, it suddenly came down. Part of the trunk hit my head on the side and the skin split and layed the skin straight down over my ear. I've had a 4-inch scar through my hair but only ½ inch of it showed on my forehead.

The first money I earned was when I took a livery team and drove a lady calling at country schools and I was to have the use of the team to go to Owens Center, 9 miles west of Rockford to call for a dance. It was the dedication of the now Woodswan Hull. They commenced to dance at nine and didn't stop until four. I got $5.00 for all day and all-night work. I got home at seven in the morning.

In March 1898, I went back to the Butcher shop to learn a trade and stayed there 6 years. The first 2 years I got $6 a week, meat and lard. Then I got $7.50, $8, and then $9 a week.

Verle was born April11, 1901.

In March 1904, I bought half interest in a butcher shop and stayed 1 year. Worked for Nobber Mills 1 year for Geo Crec and the next for J. Barelay. He had a shop at Nora Springs.

By this time I, thought farming would be better s o, I rented the Sendy Maloy farm, 7 miles S. E. of Rockford. Grace was born Oct 7, 1907. (The number 26 is written over the 7 in red ink) We stayed on this farm for 2 years. 4 years on the Archie Thompson and stayed until prosperity got to great or wonder lust. Moved to Minnesota in 1913. Lived on the P.J. Sea place for 5 years.

The family came up by train and I bought all the livestock and horses and furniture and some machinery in two boxcars. During the night, you sleep right in the boxcar with your animals. I meet family in Moorehead, 12 miles from Glyndon. It was the 4th of March and very cold. Grace got under the fur blanket or rug as they are generally called. It was some change for all of us from the milder climate of Iowa. The house on this farm was really in town. The land was on the southwest corner of the crossing of the Great Northern and Northern Pacific railroads in Glydon. Because Neve and Virgil were both in high school and Grace to enter the next fall, things were never dull at the Deach home. Someone was always there. Neve had won a piano as second prize in a contest and played really well. Just as she did everything that she ever undertook. Her scholastic rating was exceptional. Anything there was at school she was in. I had played the fiddle all my life. Verle pounded out rhythm beat with anything he could get in his hands. He even tried out the spoons on the windowpanes. So it was inevitable that he have a set of drums. He was very good to and advanced from the small country 4 or 5 piece band to one of the leading orchestra's Fargo, North Dakota. But schooling and a job put an end to that. He had a hired man at that time that could play a violin. There were always two violins on top of the piano. You could practically hear us all over town when we got to playing. Then two other boys from Downer polod Neve and Verle and played for dances. (one time in Iowa a bunch of neighbors came over to wish me happy birthday. The rug was rolled and I spent the night playing while they danced.)

Audrey was born June 7, 1915. It wasn't until she started to walk that we knew anything was wrong with her. She didn't walk until she was a year and then she just up and walked across the room but she had been hurt one side at birth. She just didn't mature fully on her foot and she was incapacitated a little on her hand. Otherwise, she is normal girl. She is with mother and I, and she sure can cook up a storm. Her buns are the tops. She can dance, boy oh boy.

In 1919, I rented a half section of hay land. Neva, Verle, Grace and myself put up 200 ton of hay. I and Neva or Verle did the mowing. Then I staked, Verle buck the hay, Neva did all the racking, and Grace drove the steaker team. Hay sold from $15 to $34 a ton. Mothers work was her onion patch and she had 300 bushels she sold them for $1.50 per bushel. Potatoes sold at a good price than too, at $1.40. Neva entered St. Theresa's at Winona the fall of 17. Verle started Fargo College the fall of 19.

We lived around Glydon for ? years. Then Verle wanted us to move closer to Crookston Minn. ER final rented the poorest farm in Polk County. I liked this particular spot. There was a little lake on the place and we actually got tired of fish. That was the nicest summer we ever had. There was not much to do. We had a few cow, chickens and pigs. You could catch a fish anytime of the day. That fall was the greatest hunting I ever had, I killed 84 pheasants, duck, etc., out of 100 shot. There was a beaver dam or the remains of one back in the woods. If you went back in the woods across a bog, you come to the loveliest bed of Moccasin flowers. I took Grace back in the woods across the bog one spring. It was very tempting not to pick a bunch of them, but I must admit now that I did pick a bouquet for mother the first time I found them.

We stayed here 2 years and then I bought a small place just south of Mentor on Maple Lake. Just one little corner of the land touched the lake. This was a nice cozy place. I had timber cut and saved for an addition to the barn. There was a very nice chicken house on the place. Mother couldn't get along without chickens and her egg money. We boiled our own maple sap here and make our own maple syrup. The woods here are full of June berry bushes and the poorest twig seemed to be loaded with them.

(My father, Elmer Deach Feb 25, 1936 wrote this for me. Mother died October 28, 1939. Father died September 28, 1942) Grace asked her father to write an autobiography of his life for her. Iowa, Minnesota, South Dakota.

THE NASHUA REPORTER, NASHUA, IOWA; BITS and Pieces; Feb 2, 1899

While Elmer Deach of Nora Springs was cutting timber an old tree fell on him, inflicting a serious scalp wound.

CLARA THERESA DEACH

Daughter of John W Deach

Clara was born May 28, 1876 in Iowa, USA.

1880 Federal Census age 4 residence Portland, Cerro Gordo, Iowa USA.

December 27, 1892 age 16 marriage to Frank Wetzel Nora Springs, Iowa, USA.

1900 Federal Census age 24 residence Washington, Carroll, Missouri, USA.

1910 Federal Census age 34 residence Washington, Carroll, Missouri, USA.

1930 Federal Census age 54 residence Washington, Carroll, Missouri, USA.

1935 age 59 residing in Washington, Carroll, Missouri, USA.

1940 Federal Census age 63 residence Washington, Carroll, Missouri, USA.

April 19, 1947 age 70 Death Braymer, Caldwell, Missouri, USA.

US., Find A Grave Index one citation provides evidence for name, birth and death.

Frank Albert Wetzel was born September 9, 1867 Dawn Livingston, Missouri, USA. and died April 19, 1953 Braymer, Missouri, USA. His parents were Lewis Wetzel and Florentine.

Frank and Clara had the following children:

(A.) LELA FLORENTINE WETZEL born November 24, 1894 Brayer, Missouri, USA. Died Sept 21, 1939 Colorado, USA.

1900 Federal Census age 6 residence Washington, Carroll, Missouri, USA.

1910 Federal Census age 16 residence Washington, Carroll, USA.

August 20 1919 age 24 married William R Davis- Livingston, Missouri, USA.

1920 Federal Census age 26 residence Fort Morgan, Colorado, USA.

1930 Federal Census age 36 Precinct 9, Boulder, Colorado, USA.

September 21, 1939 age 44 Death, Colorado, USA.

William R Davis parents were, Rees Davies and Mary.

William was born October 2, 1889, Macon, Russell Twp, Missouri, USA.

1900 Federal Census age 10 residence Lincoln, Montgomery, Iowa, USA.

Death after 1940 age 50 Colorado, USA.

1910 Federal Census age 20 residence Blue Mound, Livingston, Missouri, USA.

Lela and William had the following children:

1. Clara no date on birth but died in infancy Colorado, USA.
2. Robert Bruce Davis birth Colorado, USA. Died in childhood.
3. Donald E Davis born about 1921 Colorado, USA. Died February 14, 1979 Colorado, USA.
4. Helen Davis born about 1923 Colorado, USA.
5. Mary Kathleen Davis born October 10, 1924 Braymer, Caldwell, Missouri, USA.

1930 Federal Census, Mary age 6 residence Precinct 9, Boulder, Colorado, USA.

1935 age 11 resides Arvada, Jefferson, Colorado, USA.

1940 Federal Census age 15 Residence Arvada, Jefferson, Colorado, USA.

November 28, 1963 age 39 Death Denver, Denver Co, Colorado, USA.

Burial Denver, Denver Co, Colorado, USA.

Mary Kathleen married James Franklin Blevins January 16, 1946.

They had children five are listed private the other two are:

a. Wayne Dean (1946-1981)
b. Susan Leanne (1952-)

6.   Frank Alfred Davis born March 23, 1926 Arvada, Colorado, USA.

1930 Federal Census age 4 residence Precinct 9, Boulder, Colorado, USA.

1935 age 9 resided in Arvada, Jefferson, Colorado, USA.

1940 Federal Census age 14 residence Arvada, Jefferson, Colorado, USA.

February 23, 1957 age 30 marriage to Carolyn Elsie Claypool

1993 age 67 resides in Denver, Colorado, USA.

October 10, 2011 age 85 death Littleton, Arapahoe, Colorado, USA.

Could not find parents of Carolyn she passed in 1997. Frank and Carolyn had the following children:

1.   Brook Davis
2.   Eric Davis
3.   Penny Davis
4.   Toni Davis Sawyer
5.   T. J. Blevin

Obituary of Frank Davis;

Born March 23, 1926 Arvada, Colorado, USA. Passed away October 10, 2011. Lakewood, Co Frank Alfred Davis of Denver, 85, passed away on Oct 10, 2011 at St John's on Hospice in Lakewood. F.A. was born on Mar 23, 1926 to William and Lela Davis and raised in Arvada. He served in the Navy in WWII on the Kasaan Bay, CVE 55. He retired from Gump Glass Co.. in 1988 after working 35 years as a glazier. He was an active member of the Tyrol Ski Club where he met the love of his life

Carolyn Elsie (C.C.) Claypool. F.A. is survived by one brother, William Davis and his wife Gertrude of Golden; daughter Penny Davis of Highlands Ranch; daughter Toni Sawyer and husband Lee, along with their two children Eric and Brain of St. Joseph, Mo., a son T. J. Blevins and his two children Brook and Katie. He also leaves behind many cousins, nieces, and nephews who loved him dearly. F. A. is preceded in death by his parents; sisters Clara Madoline, Helen, Kathleen; brothers Don, Jim, and Bruce. Family was the most important thing in F. A.s life. Those that knew him will certainly miss his sense of humor, kindness, and cleverness, and his trademark Donald Duck talk. And he has left some of us wondering if being sent to the valley of Chingossles was ever really a punishment or a welcome, unexpected adventure. Oh, he sure was a good one. Services, Ft. Logan Natl. Cemetery, Tue. Oct 18. Arrive 10:45 a.m. Reception following.

7. James Edwin Davis born about 1937 Colorado, USA.

Death California, USA.

1940 Federal Census age 3 residence Arvada, Jefferson, Colorado, USA.

(B.) BEULAH L WETZEL born March 4, 1896 Missouri, USA.

1900 Federal Census age 4 residence Washington, Carroll, Missouri, USA.

1910 Federal Census age 14 residence Washington, Carroll, Missouri, USA.

1920 Federal Census age 24 residence Chillicothe Ward 3, Livingston Missouri, USA.

1930 Federal Census age 34 residence Jetmore, Hodgeman, Kansas, USA.

1956 resided in Wichita, Kansas, USA.

November 15, 1975 age 79 death Wichita, Kansas, USA.

Beulah married Robert Carl Peneiston his parents were John M Penniston 1854 and Elizabeth 1862.

They had the following children:

1. Robert C Peneiston born about 1923
2. Francis T Peneiston born about 1924
3. John M Peneiston born about 1926
4. Dan W Peneiston born about 1927
5. Shirley R Peneiston born about 1929.
6. Lila Lee born about 1934

(C.) BERNICE WETZEL born January 27, 1901 Plymouth, Missouri, USA.

1910 Federal Census age 9 residence Washington, Carroll, Missouri, USA.

December 13, 1921 age 20 marriage to George Reavis Widmeier

1930 Federal Census age 29 residence Grape Grove, Ray, Missouri, USA

1935 age 34 resided in Grape Grove, Ray, Missouri, USA.

1940 Federal Census age 39 residence Grape Grove, Ray, Missouri, USA.

July 22, 1996 age 95 death Braymer, Caldwell, Missouri, USA. Bernice is buried in Evergreen Cemetery Braymer, Caldwell County, Missouri, USA.

George Reavis Widmeier was born August 12, 1900 Braymer, Caldwell, Missouri, USA.

1910 Federal Census age 10 residence Davis, Caldwell, Missouri, USA.

1917 age 17 resided in Caldwell, Missouri, USA.31920 Federal Census age 20 residence Davis, Caldwell, Missouri, USA.

1940 Census shows his home in Grape Grove, Missouri, USA. He was the proprietor of a retail Grocery. He own his own home and made it to the 4th year of high school.

Bernice and George had the following children :

Marilyn Widmeier born July 1, 1922 Missouri, USA.

1930 Federal Census, Bern age 8 residence Grape Grove, Ray, Missouri, USA.

1935 age 13 resides in Grape Grove, Ray, Missouri, USA.

1940 Federal Census age 17 residence Grape Grove, Ray, Missouri, USA.

(D.) ANNA ESTHER WETZEL born about 1901 Missouri, USA.

1900 Residence Washington, Carroll, Missouri, USA.

1910 Federal Census age 9 residence Washington, Carroll, Missouri, USA.

June 19, 1920 age 19 marriage to Leland V North Livingston, Missouri, USA.

1930 Federal Census age 29 residence Monroe, Livingston, Missouri, USA.

1940 Federal Census age 39 residence Nodaway, Andrew, Missouri, USA.1957 resided in Kansas City, Kansas, USA.

Leland was born July 1898 Missouri, USA. parents were Clarence E North Sept 1873 and Henrietta1876.

Anna and Leland had the following children:

1. Gwendolyn R North born about 1922, Missouri, USA 1930 Federal Census age 8 residence Monroe, Livingston, Missouri, USA.
2. L Vern North born about 1923 Missouri, USA. Born March 1924 Missouri, USA.

1930 Federal Census, Vern age 6 residence Monroe, Livingston, Missouri, USA.

1935 age 11 residece New Auburn, Wisconsin, USA.

3. Roger L North born about 1928 Missouri, USA.

1930 Federal Census age 2 residence Monroe, Livingston, Missouri, USA.

1935 age 7 resides in Rural, Andrew, Missouri, USA.

1940 Federal Census age 12 residence Nodaway, Andrew, Missouri, USA.

(E.) KENNETH FRANK WETZEL born December 24, 1904 Missouri, USA.

1910 Federal Census age 6 residence Washington, Carroll, Missouri, USA.

1930 Federal Census age 26 residence Washington, Carroll, Missouri, USA.

1935 age 31 resided in Rural, Carroll, Missouri, USA.

1940 Federal Census age 35 married and residing in Washington, Carroll, Missouri, USA. Relation to head of house, Son.

May 7, 1980 age 75 death Braymer, Caldwell, Missouri, USA.

Burial Braymer, Caldwell, Missouri, USA.

Kenneth married Jewel unknown, they had the following children:

1.   Dean Wetzel born about 1929 Missouri, USA.

1935 age 6 resided in Rural, Carroll, Missouri, USA.

1940 Federal Census age 11 residence Washington, Carroll, Missouri, USA.

2.   Kenneth Wetzel born about 1929 Missouri, USA.

1930 Federal Census age 1 residence Washington, Carroll, Missouri, USA.

3.   Deloris Wetzel born about 1931 Missouri, USA.

1935 age 4 resided in Rural, Carroll, Missouri, USA.

1940 Federal Census age 9 residence Washington, Carroll, Missouri, USA.

4.   Gerald Bruce Wetzel born January 19, 1932 Missouri, USA.

1935 age 3 resided in Rural, Carroll, Missouri, USA.

October 15, 1953 marriage to Barbara Ann McKnight Braymer, Caldwell Co., Missouri, USA.

1958 age 26 resided in Silver Spring, Maryland, USA.

1984 age 52 resided in Sterling, Va., USA.

April 28, 2007 age 75 death Chesapeake Va., USA

Burial Evergreen Cemetery Braymer, Caldwell, Missouri, USA.

Barbara Ann McKnight was born September 25, 1932 Braymer, Caldwell, Missouri, USA.

November 9, 2009 age 77 death Virginia Beach, Virginia, USA.

Gerald and Barbara had the following children: Found no children for this union.

5.   Joan Wetzel born about 1933 Missouri, USA.

1935 age 2 resided Rural, Carroll, Missouri, USA.

1940 Federal Census age 7 residence Washington, Carroll, Missouri, USA.

(F.)   VELMA FRANCIS WETZEL born March 25, 1910 Braymer, Caldwell, Missouri, USA.

1930 Federal Census age 20 residence Washington, Carroll, Missouri, USA.

December 19, 1931 age 21 marriage to Norman M Bryan.

1935 age 25 residence Monroe, Livingston, Missouri, USA.

1940 Federal Census age 30 residence Monroe, Livingston, Missouri, USA.

February 2, 1998 age 87 death Chillicothe, Livingston, County, Missouri, USA.

Burial Ludlow, Livingston County, Missouri, USA.

Norman was born January 5, 1907 Livingston, Missouri, USA.

1910 Federal Census age 3 residence Monroe, Livingston, Missouri, USA.

1920 Federal Census age 13 residence Monroe, Livingston, Missouri, USA.

1930 Federal Census age 23 residence Ludlow, Livingston, Missouri, USA.

April 19, 1989 age 82 death Ludlow, Livingston, Missouri, USA.

Normans parents were Thomas A Bryan 1878-1940 and Luella Bryan 1879-1954.

I could find no children for Velma and Norman.

LILLIAN RUTH WETZEL

Daughter of John W Deach

Lillian was born November 20, 1879 Cerro Gordo, Iowa, USA.

1880 age 1 resided in Portland, Cerro Gordo, Iowa, USA.

1895 age 16 residence Nora Springs, Iowa, USA.

1910 Federal Census age 31 residence Rock Grove, Floyd, Iowa, USA.

1920 Federal Census age 41 Residence Rock Grove, Floyd, Iowa, USA.

1925 age 45 resides in Floyd, Iowa, USA.

1930 Federal Census age 51 residence Charles City, Floyd, Iowa, USA.

June 30, 1964 age 84 death Cedar Valley Hospital, Charles City, Iowa.

Burial Riverside Cemetery Iowa, Missouri, USA.

Lillian married Walter S Mathers born about 1875. His parents were William Mathers 1823-1893 and Eliza Slee 1828-1919.

Lillian and Walter had the following children:

(A.) WALTER W MATHERS born March 31, 1899 Iowa, USA.

1910 Federal Census age 11 residence Rock Grove, Floyd, Iowa, USA.

1920 Federal Census age 21 residence Rock Grove, Floyd, Iowa, USA.

1930 Federal Census age 31 residence Charles City, Floyd, Iowa, USA.

July 19, 1995 death Greenville, Mercer, Pennsylvania.

(B.) LEONARD L MATHERS born June 4, 1899 Iowa, USA.

1910 Federal Census age 11 residence Rock Grove, Floyd, Iowa, USA.

1917 age 18 resided in Floyd, Iowa, USA.

1920 Federal Census age 21 residence Rock Grove, Floyd, Iowa, USA.

January 1 1925 age 25, married residence Mitchell, Iowa, USA.

1930 Federal Census age 31 residence Clear Lake, Cerro Gordo, Iowa, USA.

1940 Federal Census age 40 residence Clear Lake Cerro Gordo, Iowa, USA.

1942 age 43 resided in Clear Lake, Iowa, USA.

September 12, 1979 age 80 death Multnomah, Oregon, USA.

Leonard married Mable E born about 1903 Iowa, USA.

Could not find parents for Mable.

Leonard and Mable had the following children:

1. Vaughn Eugene Mathers born September 30, 1923 Orchard Iowa, USA.

January 1 1925 age one residence Mitchell, Iowa, USA.

1930 Federal Census age 7 residence Clear Lake, Cerro Gordo, Iowa, USA.

1935 age 12 residence Clear Lake, Cerro Gordo, Iowa, USA.

1940 Federal Census age 16 residence Clear Lake, Cerro Gordo, Iowa, USA.

August 11 1949 age 25 residence Clear Lake, Iowa, USA.

November 30, 2007 age 84 death Multnomah Portland Oregon, USA

Could find no marriage for Vaughn.

2. WAYNE W MATHERS born about 1902 Iowa, USA.

1910 Federal Census age 8 residence Rock Grove, Floyd, Iowa, USA.

1920 Federal Census age 18 residence Rock Grove, Floyd, Iowa, USA.

1930 Federal Census age 28 residence Charles City, Floyd, Iowa, USA.

June 11, 1931 age 29 marriage to Geraldine Avis Shufelt New Hampton, Iowa, USA.

1935 age 33 residence Charles City, Floyd, Iowa, USA.

January 9, 1944 age 42 death Charles City, Floyd Iowa, USA.

Geraldine was born August 26, 1913.

Her parents were Cecil Laverne Shufelt 1891-1962 and Nellie Hazel Watkins 1894-1955.

Geraldine died April 1, 1996 at the age of 82 in Ventura, California, USA. I could find no children for this union.

3.   DORTHA H MATHERS born November 22, 1909 Iowa, USA

1910 Federal Census age 1 residence Rock Grove, Floyd, Iowa, USA.

1920 Federal Census age 11 residence Rock Grove, Floyd, Iowa USA.

1925 age 15 resided in Floyd, Iowa, USA.

July 14, 1925 marriage to Jay L Demaray

September 1983 age 73 death Floyd, Floyd, Iowa, USA

Dortha and Jay had the following children:

a.   Irwin L Demaray born Septemper 26, 1925 Floyd County, Iowa, USA.

1930 Federal Census age 5 residence Ulster, Floyd, Iowa, USA.

March 15, 1993 age 67 death Rudd, Floyd, Iowa, USA.

c. Layton C Demaray
d. Virden J Demaray

GRACE E DEACH

Daughter of John W Deach

Grace was born on February 3, 1881Portland, Floyd County, Iowa, USA

1895 age 14 residence Nora Springs, Floyd, Iowa, USA.

1900 Federal Census age 19 residence Rock Grove, Floyds, Iowa, USA.

1906 age 24 marriage to Casey J Riley.

1910 Federal Census age 29 residence Lincoln Ward 6, Lancaster, Nebraska, USA.

1911 age 30 residence Lincoln, Nebraska, USA.

1916 age 35 residence Lincoln, Nebraska, USA.

1920 Federal Census age 39 residence Hasting Ward 3, Adams, Nebraska, USA.

1930 age 49 reisdence Sheridan, Sheridan, Wyoming, USA.

1931 age 50 residence Sheridan, Wyoming, USA.

1935 age 54 residence Boone, Boone, Iowa, USA.

1940 Federal Census age 59 residence Boone, Boone, Wyoming, USA.

September 8, 1941 age 60 death Sheridan, Sheridan, Wyoming, USA.

Casey's parents were George W Riley 1842 and Martha Jane 1840.

George's occupation in 1920 was a traveling salesman for wholesale groceries.

Obituary for Grace Deach Riley;

Funeral services for Grace Deach Riley, widow of Casey J Riley, who died at the home of her daughter Mrs. James McCoy, Jr. at 1:30 Monday morning, will be held Wednesday, September 10, From the Champion Drawing room.

Mrs. Riley was born in Nora Springs, Iowa and she succumbed following an illness of about a month.

She was married January 1906 at Nora Springs. Mr. Riley preceded her in death December 22, 1939. Mr. and Mrs. Riley came to Sheridan in 1922 from Hastings, Nebraska.

She was a member of the Episcopal Church. Surviving Mrs. Riley, in addition to her daughter are three sisters, Mrs. Anna Burt, Sheridan; Mrs. Frank Wetzel, Braymer,Mo.; and Mrs. W. S. Mathers, Charles City Iowa; a brother John Deach of Mason City Iowa; and two grandchildren, James Dennis McCoy and Michael Terry McCoy, both of Sheridan. A brother, Elmer Deach, died August 20, 1941, in Menter, Minn.

The Rev. Donald G. Smith will officiate at the services Wednesday morning at ten o'clock from Champion's Drawing Room. The casket will not be opened at the services, but friends may call at the Champions between the hours of four and nine p.m. Tuesday.

Sheridan Press Sept 8, 1941

While the obit states Mr. Riley died Dec. 22, 1939, his obit was in the Sheridan Press, May 22, 1939.

Burial Sheridan Municipal Cemetery Sheridan, Sheridan County, Wyoming, USA. Plot Block 32 lot 5.

Grace and George had the following child:

(A.) Francis E Riley born about 1914.

1920 Federal Census age 6 residence Hastings Ward 3, Adams, Nebraska, USA.

1930 Federal Census age 16 residence Sheridan, Sheridan, Wyoming, USA.

Francis married James Howard McCoy born April 16, 1911 Wyoming, USA

Francis and James had the following children:

1. Michael Torrance McCoy
2. James Dennis

JOHN BRYON DEACH

Son of John W Deach

John was born September 13, 1883 South Dakota.

1895 age 12 residence Nora Springs, Floyd, Iowa, USA.

1900 Federal Census age 17 residence Rock Grove, Floyd, Iowa, USA.

October 3, 1910 age 27 marriage to Nellie M Breaky, Christian Parsonage, Charles City, Iowa, USA.

1910 Federal Census age 27 residence Rock Grove, Floyd, Iowa, USA.

1912 age 29 residence Floyd, Iowa, USA.

1917 age 34 residence Floyd, Iowa, USA.

1920 Federal Census age 37 residence Rock Grove, Floyd, Iowa, USA.

1925 age 41 residence Floyd, Iowa, USA.

1930 Federal Census age 47 Residence Cerro Gordo, Iowa, USA.

1935 age 52 residence Mason City, Cerro Gordo, Iowa, USA.

1939 age 56 residence Mason City, Iowa, USA.

1940 Federal Census, age 56 residence Mason City, Cerro Gordo, Iowa, USA.

August 19, 1948 age 64 death Clear Lake, Cerro Gordo, Iowa, USA.

Burial Mason City, Cerro Gordo, Iowa, USA.

Obituary for John B Deach;

August 21, 1948 Mason City Globe-Gazette, Mason City, Iowa Plan Rites for J. B. Deach, 64 Services at Ward's Saturday, 2:30 P.M. Clear Lake- Funeral services for John B Deach, 64, who died at his home on the north shore Wednesday evening after a long illness, will be held at Ward's Funeral home Saturday afternoon at 2:30. Burial will be in Memorial Park Cemetery. Mr. Deach had been bedfast about 14 months.

Mr. Deach was born September 13, 1884 in Spink County, South Dakota, son of John and Lucinda Deach. The family moved to Iowa when he was still a small child. He married to Miss Nellie Breaky of Nora Springs, at the Christian parsonage, Charles City, Oct 3, 1910 by Rev Burch, pastor; they have lived in this vicinity since Mr. Deach was a carpenter by trade and served as a plain-clothes policeman at Mason City and as a deputy sheriff with Jack Robinson. He was also deputy sheriff in Floyd and Mitchell counties. The Deaches had lived at Clear Lake 3 years.

Besides his wife, Mr. Deach is survived by a daughter, Mrs. Don Estle, 15 20th S.E. Mason City; five grandchildren and two sisters, Mrs. T. A. Burt, Sheridan, Wyo., and Mrs. Walter Mathers, Charles City.

He was preceded by death by his parents, a daughter Estella Marie, 21, who died 12 years ago, a brother Elmer Deach, Fisher Minn., and two sisters, Mrs. Frank Wetzel, Braymer, Mo., and Mrs. Casey Riley, Sheridan, Wyo.

Nellie was born July 4, 1891 Rudd, Floyd, Iowa, USA. Nellie died September 30, 1961 at the age of 70, Good Samaritan Home, Nora Springs, Iowa. Burial at Memorial Park Cemetery per Mason City Globe-Gazette. Nellie's parents were James Breakey and Etta Boyer.

John and Nellie had the following children:

1.   Virginia G Deach born about 1913 Iowa, USA.

1920 Federal Census age 7 residence Rock Grove, Floyd, Iowa, USA.

1925 age 12 residence Floyd, Iowa, USA.

February 20, 1930 marriage age 17, to Les Elmer Johnson Mason City, Iowa, USA.

Les Elmer Johnson was born January 18, 1903 Floyd, Iowa, USA.

1930 Federal Census age 27 residence Lake Cerro Gordo, Iowa, USA.

January 28, 1983 age 80 death St Cloud Hospital, Minnesota. Les Elmer's parents were Alfred John Johnson 1852-1914 and Emma 1871-1937.

2.   Estella Marie born about 1915 Iowa, USA. 1920 Federal Census age 5 residence Rock Grove, Floyd, Iowa, USA.

1925 age 10 resided in Floyd, Iowa, USA.

1930 Federal Census age 15 residence Lake, Cerro Gordo, Iowa, USA.

March 8, age 19 marriage to Edwin E Byerley Northwood, Worth, Iowa, USA.

Death about 1936 age 21.

ANNA RACHEL DEACH

Daughter of John W Deach

Anna Rachel Deach Born July 25, 1888 Spink, South Dakota, USA.

1900 Federal Census age 12 residence Rock Grove, Floyd, Iowa, USA.

1910 Federal Census age 22 residence Rock Grove, Floyd, Iowa, USA.

1915 age 27 residence Nora Springs, Floyd, Iowa, USA.

October 8 1925 age 37 marriage to Taylor Austin Burt Worth, Wyoming, USA.

August 1970 age 82 death Basin, Big Horn, Wyoming, USA.

Obituary Birth July 25, 1888 Iowa, USA.

Death Aug 22, 1970 Basin Big Horn County Wyoming, USA.

Mrs. Anna Burt was born July 25, 1888 in Iowa. For many years, she was a Study Hall Supervisor at Sheridan High School.

She was a member of the Friendship Chapter of The Order of Eastern Star and the Methodist Church. Survivors include one niece, Mrs. James "Frances" McCoy, Parma Heights, Ohio and several Grandnieces and Nephews. Funeral services will be held Wednesday at 2P.M. from Champion's Funeral Home with the Rev. Kenneth Rice and the Friendship Chapter of The Order of Eastern Star. Officiating. Interment will be in Sheridan Cemetery.

Mrs. Burt was a secretary to the county superintendent of schools for several years and sponsor of the 1952 graduating class of Sheridan High School. She was a member of the Wyoming Society, Christian service and the Alpha Kappa class. She was interested in youth groups both in High School and in Church.

Grace Riley owned the plot according to cemetery records.

Burial Sheridan Municipal Cemetery Sheridan, Sheridan County Wyoming, USA Plot: Block 32 lot 5

Created by Karylyn Petrie Recorded added; July 26, 2006 Find A Grave Memorial # 15051798.

Taylor Austin Burt born May 28, 1878 Nebraska, USA. June 2, 1885 age 7 resided in District M. 278, Fillmore Nebraska, USA.

Taylor's parents were Henry L Burt and Margaret E "Maggie" Gillespie.

Found no children for this union.

Clara Deach, Frank Wetzel and Family
Donated by Jo Ann Adair Granddaughter

MARY ANN DEACH

Daughter of August Deach and Martha Schultz

MARY ANN DEACH

Daughter of August Deach and Marta Schultz

Mary was born 1849 Quebec, Canada.

Marriage to John Brumpton August 8, 1870. Oxford County, Canada. About 20 years old.

1871 Census of Canada age 22 residence South Norwich, South Oxford, Ontario, Canada.

February 21, 1890 age 41 death Oxford, Ontario, Canada. Belonged to the Church of England.

In my researching Mary Deach, when she went with John to apply for their marriage license, Mary did not know the names of her parents. Her father had died in Germany and her mother entered Canada while pregnant with Mary.

John Brumpton born about 1842 Canada East, Quebec. His parents were Thomas Brumpton 1810 and Mary O'Donnell 1807-1887.

1871 Census of Canada age 29 residence South Norwich, South Oxford, Ontario, Canada.

1881 Census of Canada age 39 residence Oxford South, Ontario, Canada.

1891 Census of Canada age 49 residence Oxford South, Ontario, Canada.

1901 Census of Canada age 59 residence Norwich, Oxford, Ontario, Canada.

December 3, 1908 age 66 death Oxford, Ontario, Canada.

Mary and John had the following children:

(A.) CHARLES EDWARD BRUMPTON born December 31, 1871 Oxford, Ontario, Canada

1891 Census of Canada age 20 residence Oxford South, Ontario, Canada.

1896 age 25 arrival into the USA.

1911 Arrival Portal North Dakota, USA age 39.

1920 Federal Census age 49 residence Plentywood, Sheridan, Montana, USA.

1930 Federal Census age 59 residence Miles, Custer, Montana, USA.

February 11, 1935 death Custer, Montana, USA. Burial Miles City, Custer County, Montana, USA.

Charles married Mathilda "Tillie" Wankel date unknown. She was born November 23, 1865 in Rochester, New York, USA.

Mathilda parents were Wilhelm Blasius Josef Wankel and Julie Wilhelmine Von Taeschler.

Charles and Tillie had the following Children;

1.   Ruth Esther Brumpton born July 10, 1902 New York.

1920 Federal Census age 17 residence Plentywood, Sheridan, Montana, USA.

January 5, 1926 marriage to John Lucas- Glendive, Dawson, Montana, USA.

1930 Federal Census age 27 residence Miles, Custer, Montana, USA.

1940 Federal Census age 37 residence Miles City, Custer, Montana, USA.

February 20, 1984 Ruth age 79 death Dallas, Dallas, Texas, USA.

Buried Dallas, Dallas County, Texas, USA.

John was born January 28, 1900 Athens, Greece.

December 10 1972 John age 72 death Miles City, Custer, Montana. Buried Miles City, Custer County, Montana, USA.

Ruth and John had the following children:

1.   Paul Lucas born about 1934 Montana, USA.

1935 age 1 resides in Miles City, Custer, Montana, USA.

1940 Federal Census age 6 residence Miles City, Custer, Montana, USA.

2.   Robert Lucas born about 1936 Montana, USA.

1940 Federal Census age 4 residence Miles City, Custer, Montana, USA.

(B.)   WILLIAM BRUMPTON born about 1871 Ontario, Canada.

1879 age eight residence Ontario, Canada.

February 23 1886 age 15 marriage to Elizabeth Janet Husband Fordwich, Ontario, Canada.

(C.)   GEORGE BRUMPTON born April 4 1874 Ontario, Canada.

1891 Canada Census age 17 residence Oxford South, Ontario, Canada.

1921 Canada Census age 47 residence Delhi, Norfolk, Ontario, Canada. Married.

George was married to Margaret born about 1878.

1921 Canada Census age 47 residence Delhi, Norfolk, Ontario, Canada.

Margaret died June 5, 1931 age 53 Norfolk, Ontario, Canada.

George died April 8, 1937 age 63 death Oxford, Ontario, Canada.

George and Margaret had the following children:

1.   Edna Brumpton Born about 1902 Ontario, Canada.

1921 Canada Census age 19 residence Delhi, Norfolk, Ontario, Canada.

1949 to 1963 Edna resided in York, Ontario, Canada.

2.   Flossie Brumpton born about 1907 Ontario, Canada.

1921 Canada Census age 14 residence Delhi, Norfolk, Ontario, Canada.

August 9, 1927 age 20 marriage to Albert Earnest Dunn.

Albert Earnest Dunn was born November 24 1904 Norfolk, Ontario, Canada.

October 28, 1926 arrival Eastport, Idaho, USA.

(D.)   AMELIE THERESA BRUMPTON born August 1, 1876 Oxford, Ontario, Canada.

1881 Canada Census age 5 residence Oxford South, Ontario, CANADA.

1891 Canada Census age 15 residence Oxford South, Ontario, Canada.

August 26, 1896 age 20 marriage to Benjamin Swance- Oxford, Ontario, Canada.

1901 Canada Census age 25 residence Norwich, Oxford, Ontairo, Canada.

1911 Canada Census age 35 residence Oxford South, Ontario, Canada.

1921 Canada Census age 44 residence South Norwich, Oxford South, Ontario, Canada.

Benjamin Swance was born June 20, 1854 Haldimand Co, Ontario, Canada. Benjamin had been married prior to Amelia, which brings to reason the ages of their children.

Amelia and Benjamin had the following children:

(1.) John Alfred Swance born March 8, 1885 mothers name Nina Brown Ontario, Canada.

1901 Canada Census age 16 residence Norwich, Oxford, Ontario, Canada.

December 25, 1907 marriage to Edith M A Baxter Dereham Oxford County, Ontario, Canada.

1921 Canada Census age 36 residence Dereham, Oxford South, Ontario, Canada.

May 28, 1934 age 49 death- Oxford, Ontario, Canada.

John's wife went by the name Ada she was born about 1887 Ontario, Canada.

John and Ada had the following children:

a. Harry Edmond Swance born January 17, 1909 Oxford, Ontario, Canada.

1921 age 12 residence Dereham, Oxford South, Ontario, Canada.

Death Woodstock, Canada, date unknown

June 17, 1933 Harry married Opal Luella Holmes Elgin County, Ontario, Canada.

Opal was born November 21, 1910 Belmont Village, Elgin County, Ontario, Canada. Her parents were Miles Holms 1873-Effie Ann unknown 1873. Opal died November 10, 1982 age 71 Woodstock, Ontario, Canada.

Harry and Opal had the following children:

1. Sandra Swance birth Ontario, Canada- Death Ontario, Canada.
2. Shirley Irene Swance born May 13, 1934 Curries, Ontario, Canada.

March 11, 1997, Shirley age 62, Embro, Ontario, Canada.

3. Catherine Kay Isabella Swance born February 25, 1937 Dereham, Elgin County, Ontario, Canada.
4. Ronald Jacob Swance born July 27, 1938 Dereham, Elgin County, Ontario, Canada.

Death May 21 2013, Ronald age 74 Woodstock, Ontario, Canada.

(2.) Cora May Swance Born September 7, 1911 Oxford, Ontario, Canada.

Death age 7 Oxford, Ontario, Canada.

c. Vera Swance born about 1912 Ontario, Canada.

1921 Canada Census age 9 residence Dereham, Oxford, Ontario, Canada.

d. Floyd Swance born about 1919 Ontario, Canada.

1921 Canada Census age 2 residence Dereham, Oxford South, Ontario, Canada.

March 3, 1975 age 56 death Camden, Georgia

d. Violet Murial Swance born about 1920 Oxford County, Ontario, Canada.

1921 Canada Census age 1 residence Dereham, Oxford South, Ontario, Canada.1996 Death age 76.

(3.) Benjamin C Swance born January 15, 1890 Ontario, Canada.

1901 Canada Census age 11 residence Norwich, Oxford, Ontario, Canada.

1921 Canada Census age 31 residence North Norwich, Oxford South, Ontario, Canada.

1980 age 90 death- Tillsonburg, Ontario, Canada.

Benjamin married Annie Pearl Hughes December 4, 1917 Tillson, Ontario, Canada.

Annie was born about 1890 South Norwich Twp, Oxford County, Ontario, Canada.

Benjamin and Annie had the following children:

1.   Evelyn F Swance born about 1920 Ontario, Canada.

1921 Canada Census age 1 residence North Norwich, Oxford South, Ontario, Canada.

(4.) Gennie Swance born January 1890 Ontario, Canada.

1911 Canada Census age 21 residence Oxford South, Ontario, Canada.

(5.) Lillian Swance born November 26, 1897 Ontario, Canada.

1901 Canada Census age 4 residence Norwich, Oxford, Ontario, Canada.

1911 Canada Census age 14 residence Oxford South, Ontario, Canada.

November 27, 1918 marriage to George Washington Glover Tilsonburg, Ontario, Canada.

1921 Canada Census age 23 residence York, York West, Ontario, Canada.

1956 age 59 death. Burial Steelville, Peel County, Ontario, Canada.

George was born March 27, 1893 Cathcart, Buford Twp, Brant, Ontario, Canada.

Lillian and George had the following children:

Dorothy Glover born about 1920 Ontario, Canada.

1921 Canada Census age 1 residence York, York West, Ontario, Canada.

(6.)   Herold Swance born September 16, 1899 Oxford, Ontario, Canada.

1901 Canada Census age 2 residence Norwich, Oxford South, Ontario, Canada.

1911 Canada Census age 12 residence Oxford South, Ontario, Canada.

1921 Canada Census age 21 residence South Norwich, Oxford South, Ontario, Canada.

(7.)   Lloyd Arnold Swance born June 6, 1901 born Oxford, Ontario, Canada.

1911 Canada Census age 10 residece Oxford South, Ontario, Canada.

1921 Canada Census age 19 residence South Norwich, Oxford South, Ontario, Canada.

September 3 1933 death- Middlesex, Ontario, Canada.

(8.)   Clarence Swance Born March 30, 1904 Ontario.

1911 Canada Census age 11 residence Oxford South, Ontario, Canada.

January 16, age 21 marriage to Glady's Ecker Oxford, Ontario, Canada.

1980 age 76 death Tilsonburg, Ontario, Canada.

Gladys's was born January 25, 1903, died 1956 Ontario, Canada. Her parents were Robert Henry Ecker 1868-1940 and Sarah Amelia Bronson 1876- 1958.

Clarence and Glady's had the following children:

1. Muriel Amelia Swance born August 8, Tillsonburg, Oxford County, Ontario, Canada.

September 22, age 78 death- Ontario, Canada.

(9.)   Flossie Evelyn Swance born November 10, 1906 Oxford, Ontario, Canada

1911 Canada Census age 5 residence Oxford South, Ontario, Canada.

1921 Canada Census age 14 residence South Norwich, Oxford South, Ontario, Canada.

(10.) Mary Irene Swance born February 15, 1910 Oxford, Ontario, Canada.

1911 Canada Census age 1 residence Oxford South, Ontario, Canada.

1921 Canada Census age 11 residence South Norwich, Oxford South, Ontario, Canada.

(E.) JOHN BRUMPTON Born about 1877 Ontario, Canada.

1891 Canada Census age 14 residence Oxford South, Ontario, Canada.

1901 Canada Census age 24 residence Norwich South, Oxford, Ontario, Canada. January 28, 1919 age 42

Oxford, Ontario, Canada.

(F.) Thomas Brumpton born September 11, 1880 Otterville, Ontario, Canada.

1891 Canada Census age 11 residence Oxford South, Ontario, Canada.

1901 Canada Census age 21 residence Norwich South, Oxford South, Ontario, Canada.

April 20 1904 age 23 marriage to Mary Kienzle Oxford County, Ontario, Canada.

1921 Canada Census age 40 residence South Norwich Twp, Oxford South, Ontario, Canada.

August 13, 1925 age 44 Arrival Detroit, Wayne, Michigan, USA. Arrival contact fried Mrs. J. Horris.

1930 Federal Census age 50 residence Dearborn, Wayne, Michigan, USA.

November 15, 1932 age 52 Arrival Ontario, Canada. Citizenship American.

Mary was born about 1880, Canada. Mary cross the border into the USA. October 12 1925 arrival contact bother Ch Kinzley.

Thomas and Mary had the following Children:

1. Alvin Louis Brumpton born March 26, 1905 Oxford, Ontario, Canada.

1921 Canada Census age 16 residence South Norwich Twp, Oxford South, Ontario, Canada.

October 12, 1925 arrival Detroit, Michigan, USA. Arrival contact father.

1930 Federal Census age 25 residence Dearborn, Wayne, Michigan, USA.

November 15 1932 age 27 arrival Ontario, Canada. Citizenship American.

(G.) Elizabeth Nancy Brumpton born January 15, 1883 Oxford Ontario, Canada.

1891 Canada Census age 8 residence Oxford South, Ontario, Canada, USA.

1901 Canada Census age 18 residence Norwich South, Oxford South, Ontario, Canada.

(H.) Arthur Brumpton born August 3, 1890 Oxford Ontario, Canada.

1891 Canada Census age 1 residence Oxford South, Ontario, Canada.

1901 Canada Census age 11 residence Norwich South, Oxford South, Ontario, Canada.

December 20,1914 marriage to Jean Alberta Watson.

1921 Canada Census age 30 residence Town of Tillsonburg, Oxford South, Ontario, Canada.

Jean A Watson born August 31, 1890 Oxford, Ontario, Canada. Her parent were Joseph Shier Watson 1858-1938 and Jane Pringle 1856-

Arthur and Jean had the following children:

1.   Helen Watson Brumpton born about 1920 Ontario, Canada.

1921 Canada Census age 1 residence Town of Tillsonburg, Oxford South, Ontario, Canada.

Charles Edward Brumpton and wife Mathida Wankel
Donated by Karen Dunbrook

www.ingramcontent.com/pod-product-compliance
Lightning Source LLC
Chambersburg PA
CBHW020528290526
45786CB00002B/791